P9-DJL-066

THE
COMPLETE
WORST-CASE SCENARIO
Survival Handbook

The
COMPLETE
WORST-CASE SCENARIO
Survival Handbook

By Joshua Piven and David Borgenicht
With contributions by Jim Grace, Sarah Jordan,
Piers Marchant, and Jennifer Worick

Illustrations by Brenda Brown

CHRONICLE BOOKS
SAN FRANCISCO

Copyright © 1999–2007 by Quirk Productions, Inc.

All rights reserved. No part of this book may be reproduced in any form without written permission from the publisher.

Worst-Case Scenario® and The Worst-Case Scenario Survival Handbook™ are trademarks of Quirk Productions, Inc.

Library of Congress Cataloging-in-Publication Data available.

ISBN-13: 978-0-8118-6136-6   `

Manufactured in Canada

Designed by Bob O'Mara
Illustrations by Brenda Brown

Visit www.worstcasescenarios.com

10 9 8 7 6 5 4

Chronicle Books LLC
680 Second Street
San Francisco, California 94107
www.chroniclebooks.com

WARNING

When a life is imperiled or a dire situation is at hand, safe alternatives may not exist. To deal with the worst-case scenarios presented in this book, we highly recommend—insist, actually—that the best course of action is to consult a professionally trained expert. But because highly trained professionals may not always be available when the safety or sanity of individuals is at risk, we have asked experts on various subjects to describe the techniques they might employ in these emergency situations. THE PUBLISHER, AUTHORS, AND EXPERTS DISCLAIM ANY LIABILITY from any injury that may result from the use, proper or improper, of the information contained in this book. All the answers in this book come from experts in the situation at hand, but we do not guarantee that the information contained herein is complete, safe, or accurate, nor should it be considered a substitute for your good judgment or common sense. And finally, nothing in this book should be construed or interpreted to infringe on the rights of other persons or to violate criminal statutes; we urge you to obey all laws and respect all rights, including property rights, of others.

—The Authors

CONTENTS

Hope for the best. Expect the worst.

—Mel Brooks

INTRODUCTION

It's impossible to know exactly how many disasters we have helped people survive since we first published the original *Worst-Case Scenario Survival Handbook* back in 1999. But eleven handbooks later, we're confident that we've made people a little more prepared, and we know we've made the world at least a little safer.

The principle behind *The Worst-Case Scenario Survival Handbooks* remains a simple one: You just never know. You don't know what curves life will throw at you, what is lurking around the corner, what is hovering above, or what is swimming beneath the surface. You never know when you will be thrust into a dangerous situation and need to act fast, either to save yourself or save someone you're with.

When the time comes, we want you to know what to do, and that's why we've written these books. We want you to know what to do when the pilot passes out and you have to land the plane, when a stampede of elephants is bearing down on you, when the piranhas are restless, and when the shark fin starts heading your way. We want you to know how to deliver a baby in a taxi, how to dislodge a tongue that's been frozen to a lamppost, and how to extract your necktie from the document feeder. We want you to know how to get out of the blazing high-rise hotel and how to respond when you've woken up next to someone whose name you can't remember. We want you to know what to do in these and hundreds of other threatening situations.

And so, after years of research and writing, after consulting with experts in scores of disciplines, we've compiled all our scenarios into this fat volume and accompanying CD. It's more instructive than a first-aid handbook, more comprehensive than a military field manual, and more practical than a self-help book. *The Complete Worst-Case Scenario Survival Handbook* is the ultimate survival tool. So even though you still "just never know" what's coming around the bend, with this handy resource, at least you'll be prepared.

This printed volume includes selected scenarios from all eleven of *The Worst-Case Scenario Survival Handbooks*, and the CD-ROM (that's both Mac and PC compatible) includes all the scenarios from all the books. You'll be prepared for things you never knew you had to worry about.

Because you just never know . . .

—The Authors

CHAPTER 1
ANIMAL ENCOUNTERS

HOW TO FEND OFF A SHARK

1 Hit back.
If a shark is coming toward you or attacks you, use anything you have in your possession—a camera, probe, harpoon gun, your fist—to hit the shark's eyes or gills, which are the areas most sensitive to pain.

2 Make quick, sharp, repeated jabs in these areas.
Sharks are predators and will usually only follow through on an attack if they have the advantage, so making the shark unsure of its advantage in any way possible will increase your chances of survival. Contrary to popular opinion, the shark's nose is not the area to attack, unless you cannot reach the eyes or gills. Hitting the shark simply tells it that you are not defenseless.

How to Avoid an Attack

- Always stay in groups—sharks are more likely to attack an individual.
- Do not wander too far from shore. This isolates you and creates the additional danger of being too far from assistance.
- Avoid being in the water during darkness or twilight hours, when sharks are most active and have a competitive sensory advantage.

chapter 1: animal encounters

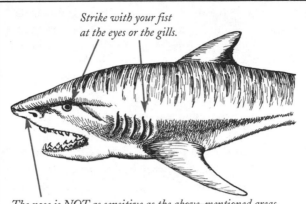

Strike with your fist at the eyes or the gills.

The nose is NOT as sensitive as the above-mentioned areas, a common misconception.

- Do not enter the water if you are bleeding from an open wound or if you are menstruating—a shark is drawn to blood and its olfactory ability is acute.
- Try not to wear shiny jewelry, because the reflected light resembles the sheen of fish scales.
- Avoid waters with known effluents or sewage and those being used by sport or commercial fishermen, especially if there are signs of bait fish or feeding activity. Diving seabirds are good indicators of such activity.
- Use extra caution when waters are murky and avoid showing any uneven tan lines or wearing brightly colored clothing—sharks see contrast particularly well.
- If a shark shows itself to you, it may be curious rather than predatory and will probably swim on

and leave you alone. If you are under the surface and lucky enough to see an attacking shark, then you do have a good chance of defending yourself if the shark is not too large.

- Scuba divers should avoid lying on the surface, where they may look like a piece of prey to a shark, and from where they cannot see a shark approaching.

- A shark attack is a potential danger for anyone who frequents marine waters, but it should be kept in perspective. Bees, wasps, and snakes are responsible for far more fatalities each year, and in the United States the annual risk of death from lightning is thirty times greater than from a shark attack.

THREE KINDS OF SHARK ATTACKS

"HIT AND RUN" ATTACKS are by far the most common. These typically occur in the surf zone, where swimmers and surfers are the targets. The victim seldom sees its attacker, and the shark does not return after inflicting a single bite or slash wound.

"BUMP AND BITE" ATTACKS are characterized by the shark initially circling and often bumping the victim prior to the actual attack. These types of attacks usually involve divers or swimmers in deeper waters, but also occur in nearshore shallows in some areas of the world.

"SNEAK" ATTACKS differ: the strike can occur without warning. With both "bump and bite" and "sneak" attacks, repeat attacks are common and multiple and sustained bites are the norm. Injuries incurred during this type of attack are usually quite severe, frequently resulting in death.

Be Aware

Most shark attacks occur in nearshore waters, typically inshore of a sandbar or between sandbars where sharks feed and can become trapped at low tide. Areas with steep drop-offs are also likely attack sites. Sharks congregate in these areas, because their natural prey congregates there. Almost any large shark, roughly six feet or longer in total length, is a potential threat to humans. But three species in particular have repeatedly attacked man: the white shark *(Carcharodon carcharias)*, the tiger shark *(Galeocerdo cuvieri)*, and the bull shark *(Carcharhinus leucas)*. All are cosmopolitan in distribution, reach large sizes, and consume large prey such as marine mammals, sea turtles, and fish as normal elements of their diets.

How to Deal with Escaped Lobsters

Close kitchen doors and cabinets to cut off escape routes. Wear oven mitts to protect you from the lobsters' pincers. Use a pot lid to herd the lobsters. Grasp each by the body from behind and place in a large, lidded pot of water, claws first.

HOW TO ESCAPE FROM A GIANT OCTOPUS

1 Pull away quickly.
In many cases, a human can escape from the grasp of a small- to medium-sized octopus by just swimming away. Propel yourself forward to create a pulling pressure on the octopus's arms. If you cannot get away, or if you feel yourself being pulled back, continue to the next step.

2 Do not go limp.
Octopi are naturally curious and, if strong enough, will check to see if you are a food item before letting you go. Do not act passively, or you may be bitten or quickly enveloped by the octopus's web, a flexible sheath used to trap prey. Once you are caught in a "web-over," escape will be extremely difficult. However, octopi tire easily, so continue to put pressure on the arms by attempting to swim away. The octopus may decide to let you go rather than bring you in for a closer look.

3 Prevent the octopus's arms from wrapping around your arms.
Initially, the octopus will secure itself to a rock or coral formation and reach out to grab you with just one or two arms. Once it has a firm grip on you, it

will move you toward its mouth (called a "beak") by transferring you to the next sucker up the arm. Do not allow the first two octopus arms to pin your own arms to your sides, or you will have little chance of fighting it off.

4 | Peel the suckers from your body.
Using your hands, start at the tip of each octopus arm and remove each successive sucker from your body, like peeling up a bath mat. Once you have loosened one of the octopus's arms, give it a spear, raft, surfboard, or other object to latch on to. Work quickly, before the suckers reattach to your body or the octopus's other arms have a chance to grab you.

5 | Detach the octopus from its anchor.
Using the sucker removal method described in step 4, separate the octopus from its anchor. Octopi prefer to be anchored to a fixed object, and may swim away once dislodged.

6 | Turn somersaults in the water.
If you have detached the octopus from its mooring but are still being held, turn your body in circles in the water to irritate it into releasing you.

7 | Swim toward the surface.
Octopi dislike air intensely and will release you once they break the surface. Continue to peel the octopus's suckers from your body as you swim.

Peel the suckers starting from the tip of the octopus's arm.

Be Aware

- A giant Pacific octopus may be well over 100 pounds, with an arm span of 23 feet.
- Giant octopi are extremely strong, but do not constrict prey to kill: They tear victims with their sharp beaks.
- Giant Pacific octopi are not poisonous, though bites may become infected.
- Octopi typically eat crabs and clams, though they may eat fish and birds, and may bite at anything.
- Without training or free-diving experience, a swimmer will typically be able to hold his or her breath for only about a minute before losing consciousness.

How to Free Your Fish If Stuck in Tank Decorations

Gently push the fish from the rear using a fish net until it is able to swim free of the obstruction. If fish is still stuck, hold the decoration just above the tank and push the fish gently out and back into the water using a wet net.

HOW TO SURVIVE A POISONOUS SNAKE ATTACK

Because poisonous snakes can be difficult to identify—and because some nonpoisonous snakes have markings very similar to venomous ones—the best way to avoid getting bitten is to leave all snakes alone. Assume that a snake is venomous unless you know for certain that it is not.

How to Treat a Bite

1 Wash the bite with soap and water as soon as you can.

2 Immobilize the bitten area and keep it lower than the heart.
This will slow the flow of the venom.

3 Get medical help as soon as possible.
A doctor should treat all snakebites unless you are willing to bet your life that the offending snake is nonpoisonous. Of about eight thousand venomous bites a year in the U.S., nine to fifteen victims are killed. A bite from any type of poisonous snake should always be considered a medical emergency. Even bites from nonpoisonous snakes should be treated professionally, as severe allergic reactions can occur. Some Mojave

rattlesnakes carry a neurotoxic venom that can affect the brain or spinal cord, causing paralysis.

4 Immediately wrap a bandage tightly two to four inches above the bite to help slow the venom if you are unable to reach medical care within thirty minutes. The bandage should not cut off blood flow from a vein or artery. Make the bandage loose enough for a finger to slip underneath.

5 If you have a first aid kit equipped with a suction device, follow the instructions for helping to draw venom out of the wound without making an incision. Generally, you will need to place the rubber suction cup over the wound and attempt to draw the venom out from the bite marks.

WHAT NOT TO DO

- Do not place any ice or cooling element on the bite; this will make removing the venom with suction more difficult.
- Do not tie a bandage or a tourniquet too tightly. If used incorrectly, a tourniquet can cut blood flow completely and damage the limb.
- Do not make any incision on or around the wound in an attempt to remove the venom—there is danger of infection.
- Do not attempt to suck out the venom. You do not want it in your mouth, where it might enter your bloodstream.

Snakes coil before they strike.

Snakes can strike at a distance approximately half their length; half their body does not leave the ground.

How to Escape from a Python

Unlike poisonous snakes, pythons and boas kill their prey not through the injection of venom but by constriction; hence these snakes are known as constrictors. A constrictor coils its body around its prey, squeezing it until the pressure is great enough to kill.

Since pythons and boas can grow to be nearly twenty feet long, they are fully capable of killing a grown person, and small children are even more vulnerable. The good news is that most pythons will strike and then try to get away, rather than consume a full-grown human.

1 Remain still.
This will minimize constriction strength, but a
python usually continues constricting well after the
prey is dead and not moving.

2 Try to control the python's head and try to
unwrap the coils, starting from whichever end
is available.

How to Avoid an Attack

- Do not try to get a closer look, prod the snake to
  make it move, or try to kill it.
- If you come across a snake, back away slowly and
  give it a wide berth: snakes can easily strike half
  their body length in an instant, and some species
  are six feet or longer.
- When hiking in an area with poisonous snakes,
  always wear thick leather boots and long pants.
- Keep to marked trails.
- Snakes are cold-blooded and need the sun to
  help regulate their body temperature. They are
  often found lying on warm rocks or in other
  sunny places.

How to Deal with a Bird Trapped in Your House

Use a broom to gently maneuver the bird into a room with a window and a door. Open the window, leave the room, and close the door. Wait for the bird to fly out. This method also works for stray squirrels.

How to Detangle a Bird
Caught in Your Hair

Shield your eyes and face with your arm. With your other hand, grab the bird's feet and legs from behind, pull it from your hair, and toss the bird lightly away from you. Do not attempt to grab the head or beak.

HOW TO
ESCAPE FROM
A MOUNTAIN LION

1 Do not run.
The animal most likely will have seen and smelled you already, and running will simply cause it to pay more attention.

2 Try to make yourself appear bigger by opening your coat wide.
The mountain lion is less likely to attack a larger animal.

3 Do not crouch down.
Hold your ground, wave your hands, and shout. Show it that you are not defenseless.

4 If you have small children with you, pick them up— do all you can to appear larger.
Children, who move quickly and have high-pitched voices, are at higher risk than adults.

5 Back away slowly or wait until the animal moves away.
Report any lion sightings to authorities as soon as possible.

Upon sighting a mountain lion, do not run.
Do not crouch down. Try to make yourself appear
larger by opening wide your coat.

6 If the lion still behaves aggressively, throw stones. Convince the lion that you are not prey and that you may be dangerous yourself.

7 Fight back if you are attacked.
Most mountain lions are small enough that an average-size human will be able to ward off an attack by fighting back aggressively. Hit the mountain lion in the head, especially around the eyes and mouth. Use sticks, fists, or whatever is at hand. Do not curl up and play dead. Mountain lions generally leap down upon prey from above and deliver a "killing bite" to the back of the neck. Their technique is to break the neck and knock down the prey, and they also will rush and lunge up at the neck of prey, dragging the victim down while holding the neck in a crushing grip. Protect your neck and throat at all costs.

How to Avoid an Attack

Mountain lions, also called cougars, have been known to attack people without provocation; aggressive ones have attacked hikers and especially small children, resulting in serious injury. Still, most mountain lions will avoid people. To minimize your contact with cougars in an area inhabited by them, avoid hiking alone and at dusk and dawn, when mountain lions are more active.

HOW TO WRESTLE FREE FROM AN ALLIGATOR

1 If you are on land, try to get on the alligator's back and put downward pressure on its neck.
This will force its head and jaws down.

2 Cover the alligator's eyes.
This will usually make it more sedate.

3 If you are attacked, go for the eyes and nose.
Use any weapon you have, or your fist.

4 If its jaws are closed on something you want to remove (for example, a limb), tap or punch it on the snout.
Alligators often open their mouths when tapped lightly. They may drop whatever it is they have taken hold of, and back off.

5 If the alligator gets you in its jaws, you must prevent it from shaking you or from rolling over—these instinctual actions cause severe tissue damage.
Try to keep the mouth clamped shut so the alligator does not begin shaking.

6 Seek medical attention immediately, even for a small cut or bruise, to treat infection.
Alligators have a huge number of pathogens in their mouths.

chapter 1: animal encounters

To get an alligator to release something it has in its mouth, tap it on the snout.

How to Avoid an Attack

While deaths in the United States from alligator attacks are rare, there are thousands of attacks and hundreds of fatalities from Nile crocodiles in Africa and Indopacific crocodiles in Asia and Australia. A few tips to keep in mind:

- Do not swim or wade in areas alligators are known to inhabit (in Florida, this can be anywhere).
- Do not swim or wade alone, and always check out the area before venturing in.
- Never feed alligators.
- Do not dangle arms and legs from boats, and avoid throwing unused bait or fish from a boat or dock.

- Do not harass, try to touch, or capture any alligator.
- Leave babies and eggs alone. Any adult alligator will respond to a distress call from any youngster. Mother alligators guarding nests and babies will defend them.
- In most cases the attacking alligators had been fed by humans prior to the attack. This is an important link—feeding alligators seems to cause them to lose their fear of humans and become more aggressive.

HOW TO DEAL WITH AN ALLIGATOR NEAR YOUR GOLF BALL

1 Determine the size of the alligator.
Although even small alligators can cause injury, those less than four feet long are not as dangerous to humans. If the alligator is larger than six feet, be especially wary, as a bite can inflict major damage. Alligators larger than nine feet should be considered deadly.

2 Calculate the distance from the alligator to your ball.
The immediate danger zone is within 15 feet of an alligator.

3 Try to determine if the alligator sees your ball.
Alligators are attracted to objects that appear to be food. Golf balls look like alligator eggs, which alligators eat.

4 Do not stand between the alligator and water.
If disturbed, an alligator on land will seek refuge in water. Make sure the alligator is between you and any nearby water hazard.

5 Make a loud noise.
Alligators are sensitive to loud noises. Yelling or screaming may cause the animal to leave. If the alligator does not move, however, you will have gained its attention.

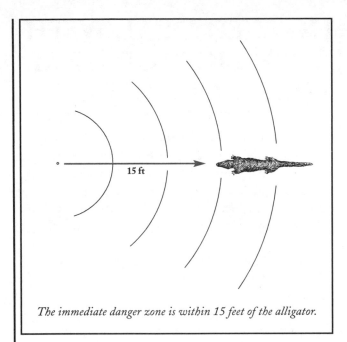

The immediate danger zone is within 15 feet of the alligator.

6 Use a ball retriever to recover the ball.
The alligator may lunge and bite at objects that invade its space. A telescoping ball retriever, best used when the alligator is not facing you or the ball, can quietly scoop up the ball. You can also use a flagstick, though you will have to use it to roll the ball out of the way.

7 Quickly move away from the alligator's territory.
After retrieving the ball, or if you encounter difficulties, run. While alligators can move fast, they generally will travel only short distances and probably cannot outrun an adult golfer.

Be Aware

- Alligators are common on golf courses throughout the Gulf Coast states in the United States, and can be found as far north as North Carolina. To be safe, assume that any body of water on a course in these states is home to an alligator.

- Never wade into a water hazard on a golf course known to be home to alligators. You are most likely to be attacked in or at the edge of water.

- Be especially wary during spring months, when alligators wander in search of mates, and during late summer, when eggs hatch. Mother alligators will respond aggressively to threats to their young, and any adult alligator may come to the aid of any youngster.

- An alligator more than nine feet long is likely to be male, and males tend to move around more and be more aggressive.

- Do not assume any alligator is safe to approach. While some animals may be habituated to the presence of humans, alligators are wild animals, and therefore unpredictable: they may attack without provocation.

how to deal with an alligator near your golf ball

HOW TO SURVIVE
AN ELEPHANT
STAMPEDE

★ Take available cover.
Elephants stampede when they are startled by a loud
noise or to escape a perceived threat. If the elephants
are running away from a threat but toward you, do not
try to outrun them. Elephants can run at a speed in
excess of 25 mph. Even while charging, they can make
sharp turns and are able to climb steep slopes. Seek a
sturdy structure close by and take cover.

★ Climb a tree.
The elephants are likely to avoid trees when running.
Grab a branch at its base and use your legs to power
yourself up the tree, keeping three of your limbs in
contact with the tree at all times as you climb. If you
cannot climb the tree, stand behind it. Elephants will
avoid large obstacles when running.

★ Lie down.
Unless the elephant is intent on trampling you,
because you are hunting or the elephant thinks you
are hunting, elephants typically avoid stepping on a
prone human being, even while charging.

chapter 1: animal encounters

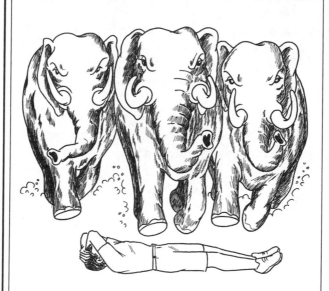

If you cannot find cover, lie down. Elephants typically avoid stepping on a prone human being, even while charging.

⭐ **Protect your face.**

Do not get up immediately. After the threat has passed, an elephant may show great interest in the apparently dead bodies of humans and may attempt to "bury" you under tree branches, leaves, and dirt. If you sense an elephant moving above you, lie still and cover your face with your hands. The rough skin on the elephant's trunk may cause severe abrasions if it rubs against you.

Be Aware

- An angry elephant will tuck its ears back and curl its trunk up, away from danger.
- If the elephants are angry at you, they may attempt to spear you with their tusks and then fling your body.
- If the last human the elephant met was a hunter/poacher, it will be more likely to treat you as a threat and attempt an attack.

How to Escape from a Stampede of Giraffes

Wade into the nearest body of water. Giraffes typically avoid water except for drinking. If you cannot reach water, climb a tree or seek available shelter. The giraffes' large hooves pose your most immediate danger.

HOW TO
ESCAPE FROM A
CHARGING RHINO

⭐ **Climb a tree.**
See "How to Survive an Elephant Stampede," on page 48.

⭐ **Run for scrub.**
A rhino probably will not follow you into thick scrub brush. Get as far in as possible. Adrenaline will prevent you from noticing the painful thorns until you try to get out.

⭐ **Stand your ground and shout.**
If no tree or scrub is available to allow your escape, stand and face the animal (rhinos have poor eyesight but are attracted to movement). As the rhino approaches, scream and shout as loud as you can. A charging rhino may veer away from a noisy target.

⭐ **Run in the opposite direction.**
A rhino will continue running in the same direction when it is charging and is not likely to turn around and come back for another attack. Once you have evaded the charge and the rhino has veered off, run in the opposite direction.

A charging rhino may avoid a noisy target.

Be Aware

- A surprised or startled rhino's first instinct is to charge a threat, whether real or imagined.
- A mother rhino will aggressively defend a calf by charging any and all threats.
- Rhinos can climb steep slopes and will also charge into water or mud.
- A rhino will charge and attack a vehicle and may chase one for more than a mile. A large male (5,000 pounds or more) can easily knock over a car.
- African black rhinos are generally considered the most dangerous and likely to charge, though white and Indian rhinos will also charge. Javan and Sumatran rhinos are smaller, shier, forest-dwelling, and considered less dangerous to humans.
- A white rhino's anterior (front) horn can be as long as 62 inches.

HOW TO CONTROL
A RUNAWAY CAMEL

1 Hang on to the reins—but do not pull them back
hard in an attempt to stop the camel.

A camel's head, unlike that of a wayward horse, cannot always be pulled to the side to slow it down.
Camels are usually harnessed with a head halter or
nose reins, and pulling on the nose reins can tear the
camel's nose—or break the reins.

*Hang on tight and
pull the reins to one side
to make the camel run in a circle.
It will stop on its own.*

2 If the camel has sturdy reins and a head halter, pull the reins to one side to make the camel run in a circle.

Do not fight the camel; pull the reins in the direction the camel attempts to turn its head. The camel may change direction several times during the incident—let it do so.

3 If the camel has nose reins, just hang on tight.

Use the reins for balance, and grip with your legs. If there is a saddle, hold on to the horn.

4 Hold on until the camel stops.

Whether the camel is running in circles or in a straight path, it will not run very far. The camel will sit down when it grows tired.

5 When the camel sits, jump off.

Hold on to the reins to keep it from running off.

How to Deal with a Deer in Your Headlights

Brake firmly and blow your horn with one long blast to frighten the deer into action. Do not swerve or you will confuse the deer about which way to run. If you hit the deer, do not touch the animal; move the car off the road, set the hazard lights, and call the police. Drive using high beams whenever possible on dark wooded roads.

HOW TO FEND OFF A CHARGING REINDEER

1 Stand your ground.

Most reindeer have been bred to be docile livestock; they are sometimes referred to as "tundra cows." They will run around, rather than over, a standing person, even when charging in a herd.

2 Watch for reindeer in rut.

Reindeer mate from late August to October, when they will be in rut, or heat, and much more dangerous. Each male, or bull, will keep a harem of females and will become unpredictable and aggressive with any person who approaches. While both male and female reindeer have antlers, male reindeer are noticeably larger, weighing 400 pounds or more. During rut, necks on males will be large and swollen.

3 Watch for front-leg kicking.

When disturbed, reindeer will rear up on the hind legs and kick out with the front hooves. Females are generally not dangerous except when defending calves. Stay well back and to the side to avoid being kicked. During rut, reindeer bulls will try to gore rather than kick, if antagonized.

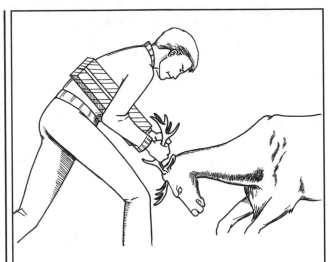

Stand your ground. Grab the reindeer by the antlers and direct its charge away from you.

4 **Watch for antler display.**
Before goring, a male will often attempt to intimidate by showing, or "presenting," its antlers, turning his head to the side. Be wary in approaching or cornering a bull reindeer during this display.

5 **Back up slowly.**
Speak to the reindeer in a soft voice. Do not make any sudden movements.

6 **Do not raise your arms over your head.**
The bull may take this as a challenge sign that you are also displaying antlers.

7 If the reindeer attempts to gore you, grab the antlers.

Grasp one branch with each hand and attempt to steer the head away from you. If the reindeer tries to lunge forward, you may not be able to stop it, but guiding the antlers may allow you to redirect its charge.

8 Move to the side quickly as you release the antlers.

The reindeer will now be beside you and may just move away. Do not run, or you will call attention to yourself. Carefully put distance between yourself and the reindeer.

9 Call for help.

Using a voice and tone that does not further antagonize the reindeer, advise others in the area of your situation. They may be able to distract the reindeer, if it is still in pursuit.

Be Aware

- Caribou, which are much more aggressive and dangerous, are often mistaken for reindeer. Reindeer have shorter legs and are rounder.
- Male reindeer have huge antlers, with as many as 14 to 18 points per side.

How to Protect Your Dog in a Sudden Rainstorm

Cut or tear holes in a plastic shopping bag for the dog's paws, head, and tail. Use a kitchen- or yard-sized bag for larger breeds. Carefully slip the bag over the dog's head and ease the front paws, back paws, and tail through the holes.

Tie the bag handles behind the tail hole for added security.

HOW TO REMOVE A TICK

Because you will probably not feel a tick biting you, it's a good practice to check yourself for ticks thoroughly after spending time outdoors.

1 **Locate the tick.**

Look for a small bump on the skin, similar to the last remnants of a scab before it heals. Ticks vary in size from the head of a pin to a fingernail (when they are engorged) depending on the type and the stage of maturity. Ticks are usually brown or reddish. Check behind the knee, between fingers and toes, in the underarms, in the belly button, in and behind the ear, on the neck, in the hairline, and on the top of the head.

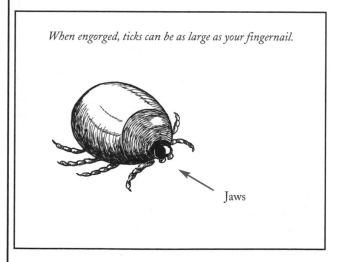

When engorged, ticks can be as large as your fingernail.

Jaws

2 | **Act quickly to remove the tick.**
Use a commercially available tick removal tool if one is available. Follow the instructions that come with the device. If no tick removal device is available, locate a pair of medium- or fine-tipped tweezers.

3 | **Place the tip of the tweezers around the area where the jaws of the tick enter the skin.**
Using a slow, steady motion, pull the tick away from the skin. Do not jerk, crush, squeeze, or puncture the tick, because more pathogens from the tick may get into the wound. If part of the tick breaks off, try to remove it as you would a splinter. Your body will naturally eject the foreign material over time, so leave it alone if you cannot remove it easily.

Place the tweezers around the tick where its jaws enter the skin. Pull with a slow, steady motion.

4 | If no tweezers are available, use the nails of your index finger and thumb.

Avoid touching the tick with your skin; use latex gloves, plastic baggies, or even paper towels to cover the skin of your fingers. If nothing to protect your skin is available, try using two credit cards as tweezers: squeeze the edges together to grab the tick and then pull firmly away from the skin. Failing this, it is better to remove the tick with bare forefinger and thumb than to leave it attached.

5 | Immediately disinfect the area around the bite with soap and water, alcohol, or antibacterial ointment.

6 | Place the tick, dead or alive, in a sealable container. Include a lightly moistened paper towel. Take the tick to a local health department to be analyzed, to determine if it is carrying disease.

How to Recognize Lyme Disease

Watch for these symptoms:
- A round, "bull's-eye" rash on the skin, which may be very small or up to twelve inches across.
- Other rashes or skin bruising that can mimic common skin problems, including hives, eczema, sunburn, poison ivy, and flea bites. The rash may itch or feel hot, and it may disappear and return several weeks later. The rash will look like a bruise on people with dark skin color.

- Flu-like symptoms several days or weeks after a bite from an infected tick: aches and pains in the muscles and joints, low-grade fever, and fatigue.
- Other systemic symptoms, which can affect virtually any organ in the body, including jaw pain and difficulty chewing; frequent or painful urination and/or repeated urinary tract infections; respiratory infection, cough, asthma, and pneumonia; ear pain, hearing loss, ringing, sensitivity to noise; sore throat, swollen glands, cough, hoarseness, difficulty swallowing; headaches, facial paralysis, seizures, meningitis, stiff neck; burning, tingling, or prickling sensations; loss of reflexes, loss of coordination; stomach pain, diarrhea, nausea, vomiting, abdominal cramps, loss of appetite; and irregular heartbeat, palpitations, fainting, shortness of breath, and chest pain.

Be Aware

- Tucking your pants into your socks is a good preventive measure against ticks.
- Ticks do not drop from high vegetation or trees; they climb up your body, generally seeking the highest point on the body. However, if the tick meets resistance, it will stop and feed at that point.
- Ticks are most active in the spring and early summer, though they may be present at other times of the year.
- Ticks are found in virtually all climates and geographic regions, from the Antarctic to the Sahara. They will often be most abundant in areas with wildlife, whose blood provides their food supply.

- On the golf course, stay on the fairway and out of the rough to avoid ticks.
- Ticks can be difficult to remove, and improper removal can cause tick mouthparts to remain in the skin and/or pathogens from the tick's body to enter the bloodstream. In particular, small, immature ticks (called larvae or nymphs) can be very hard to remove in one piece.
- Lyme disease is treatable with antibiotics—and the sooner treatment begins, the better.

How to Save Your Cat from Choking

Kneel and hold the cat in front of you, close to your chest. Place one forearm under the cat's front legs and hold him up and out-stretched, facing away from you. Place the fist of your other hand just below the bottom rib. Give 2 or 3 quick, firm pushes inward to force the air out of the diaphragm and dislodge the object.

HOW TO ESCAPE FROM AN ANGRY GORILLA

1 | Evaluate the gorilla's behavior.
A stressed or angry gorilla is likely to vocalize loudly and pound, jump, or slap the ground before attacking. A gorilla that is just tugging at clothes or grabbing at you may simply be curious.

2 | Do not react.
Do not scream, hit, or otherwise antagonize the gorilla. Even if the gorilla grabs you, it may be playful behavior. Scaring or aggravating the gorilla may provoke an angry response.

3 | Be submissive.
Do not look directly at the gorilla. Remain quiet. Do not shout or open arms wide to try to appear larger. The gorilla may interpret these acts as hostile.

4 | Watch for a bluff charge.
A gorilla may make a "bluff charge" before an attack to scare potential threats. It may scream or "bark," stomp its hands on the ground, and tear at vegetation as it advances toward you. A bluff charge is fast and intimidating and resembles an actual attack.

Groom the gorilla's arm to relax its grip.

5 Crouch down and make yourself as small a target as possible.
If the gorilla feels threatened during a bluffing display, it may decide to follow through with an attack.

6 Stay quiet and submissive.
An attack may include severe biting and pounding or tearing with the gorilla's hands. Even if it appears that the gorilla means to harm you, do not actively resist or fight back: It will interpret this behavior as threatening and may attack more severely.

7 | Groom.

If the gorilla has gotten hold of you, begin to "groom" its arm while loudly smacking your lips. Primates are fastidious groomers, and grooming the gorilla in this fashion may distract the gorilla in a nonthreatening way. As the gorilla's grip relaxes, slowly move your grooming hand to the gorilla's hand, showing keen interest in any bits of leaf or dirt on the gorilla.

8 | Remain quiet and passive until the gorilla loses interest or until help arrives.

Be Aware

If the gorilla has you in its grip, do not attempt to pry the gorilla's fingers apart to remove his hand. A full-grown silverback gorilla is much stronger than any adult human. The gorilla's grip will be like a vise that is impossible to open.

HOW TO ESCAPE FROM A BEAR

1 Lie still and quiet.
Documented attacks show that an attack by a mother black bear often ends when the person stops fighting.

2 Stay where you are and do not climb a tree to escape a bear.
Black bears can climb trees quickly and easily and will come after you. The odds are that the bear will leave you alone if you stay put.

3 If you are lying still and the bear attacks, strike back with anything you can.
Go for the bear's eyes or its snout.

WHAT TO DO IF YOU SEE A BEAR

- Make your presence known by talking loudly, clapping, singing, or occasionally calling out. (Some people prefer to wear bells.) Whatever you do, be heard—it does not pay to surprise a bear.
- Keep children close at hand and within sight.
- There is no guaranteed minimum safe distance from a bear: the farther, the better. Remember, bears can run much faster than humans.
- If you are in a car, remain in your vehicle. Do not get out, even for a quick photo. Keep your windows up. Do not impede the bear from crossing the road.

While all bears are dangerous, these three situations render even more of a threat.

Females protecting cubs.

Bears habituated to human food.

Bears defending a fresh kill.

How to Avoid an Attack

- Reduce or eliminate food odors from yourself, your camp, your clothes, and your vehicle.
- Do not sleep in the same clothes you cook in.
- Store food so that bears cannot smell or reach it.
- Do not keep food in your tent—not even a chocolate bar.
- Properly store and bring out all garbage.
- Handle and store pet food with as much care as your own.
- While all bears should be considered dangerous and should be avoided, three types should be regarded as more dangerous than the average bear. These are:

  Females defending cubs.
  Bears habituated to human food.
  Bears defending a fresh kill.

Be Aware

- There are about 650,000 black bears in North America, and only one person every three years is killed by a bear—although there are hundreds of thousands of encounters. Most bears in the continental U.S. are black bears, but black bears are not always black in color: sometimes their fur is brown or blond. Males are generally bigger than females (125 to 500 pounds for males, 90 to 300 pounds for females).

- Bears can run as fast as horses, uphill or downhill.
- Bears can climb trees, although black bears are better tree-climbers than grizzly bears.
- Bears have excellent senses of smell and hearing.
- Bears are extremely strong. They can tear cars apart looking for food.
- Every bear defends a "personal space." The extent of this space will vary with each bear and each situation; it may be a few meters or a few hundred meters. Intrusion into this space is considered a threat and may provoke an attack.
- Bears aggressively defend their food.
- All female bears defend their cubs. If a female with cubs is surprised at close range or is separated from her cubs, she may attack.
- An aggressive reaction to any danger to her cubs is the mother grizzly's natural defense.
- A female black bear's natural defense is to chase her cubs up a tree and defend them from the base.
- Stay away from dead animals. Bears may attack to defend such food.
- It is best not to hike with dogs, as dogs can antagonize bears and cause an attack. An unleashed dog may even bring a bear back to you.

HOW TO ESCAPE
FROM KILLER BEES

1 If bees begin flying around and/or stinging you,
do not freeze.
Run away; swatting at the bees only makes them
angrier.

2 Get indoors as fast as you can.

3 If no shelter is available, run through bushes
or high weeds.
This will help give you cover.

4 If a bee stings you, it will leave its stinger in
your skin.
Remove the stinger by raking your fingernail across
it in a sideways motion. Do not pinch or pull the
stinger out—this may squeeze more venom from the
stinger into your body. Do not let stingers remain in
the skin, because venom can continue to pump into
the body for up to ten minutes.

5 Do not jump into a swimming pool or other body of
water—the bees are likely to be waiting for you
when you surface.

chapter 1: animal encounters

If bees begin flying around and /or stinging you,
DO NOT freeze; DO NOT swat them. Run away.
If no shelter is available, run through bushes or high weeds.

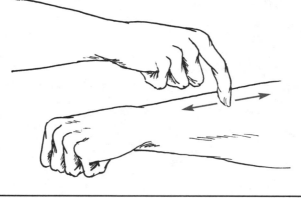

If a bee stings you, remove the stinger by raking your fingernail across it in a sideways motion. Do not pinch the area.

Risk of Attack

The Africanized honeybee is a cousin of the run-of-the-mill domesticated honeybee that has lived in the United States for centuries. The "killer bee" moniker was created after some magazine reports about several deaths that resulted from Africanized bee stings some years back. Africanized honeybees are considered "wild"; they are easily angered by animals and people, and likely to become aggressive.

Bees "swarm" most often in the spring and fall. This is when the entire colony moves to establish a new hive. They may move in large masses—called swarms—until they find a suitable spot. Once the colony is built and the bees begin raising their young, they will protect their hive by stinging.

While any colony of bees will defend its hive, Africanized bees do so with gusto. These bees can kill, and they present a danger even to those who are not allergic to bee stings. In several isolated instances, people and animals have been stung to death. Regular honeybees will chase you about fifty yards. Africanized honeybees may pursue you three times that distance.

Most often, death from stings occurs when people are not able to get away from the bees quickly. Animal losses have occurred for the same reasons— pets and livestock were tied up or penned when they encountered the bees and could not escape.

To Minimize Risk

- Avoid colonies by filling in holes or cracks in exterior walls, filling in tree cavities, and putting screens on the tops of rainspouts and over water meter boxes in the ground.
- Do not bother bee colonies: if you see that bees are building—or have already built—a colony around your home, do not disturb them. Call a pest control center to find out who removes bees.

HOW TO CATCH FISH WITHOUT A ROD

1 Determine the best location for your fishing.
Fish usually congregate in shadow, near the edges of lakes, rivers, and streams.

2 Find a forked sapling approximately two feet long. (The forked ends should be approximately one foot long.)
Cut it down or break it off.

3 Bend the two ends toward each other and tie them together.
The tied ends will form the circular frame of a net.

4 Remove your shirt or T-shirt.

5 Tie a knot in the shirt just below the arm and neck holes.

6 Slip the sapling into the shirt, and pin or tie the shirt securely to all sides of the frame.

7 Scoop up the fish.

Alternative
Large fish can also be speared with a pole sharpened to a point at one end. This method works best at night, when fish come to the surface.

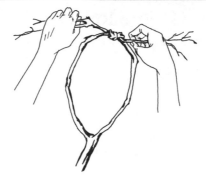

Find a forked branch. Tie the ends together.

Tie a shirt into a knot.

Slip the branch into the shirt; secure the shirt to the frame.

How to Remove a Fishhook from Flesh

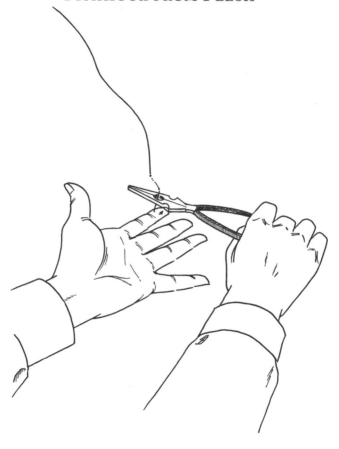

Clip off the end of the hook with a pair of needle-nose pliers. Pull the unbarbed end of the hook through the wound to remove. Apply antiseptic and dress the injury site.

HOW TO REMOVE
A LEECH

1 Do not attempt to remove a leech by pulling up on its middle section or by using salt, heat, or insect repellent.

Dislodging by squeezing, salting, burning, or otherwise annoying the leech while it is feeding will cause it to regurgitate, most likely spreading the bacteria from its digestive system into your open wound, causing infection.

2 Identify the anterior (oral) sucker.

Look for the small end of the leech. A common mistake is to go immediately to the large sucker.

3 Place a fingernail on your skin (not on the leech itself), directly adjacent to the oral sucker.

4 Gently but firmly slide your finger toward where the leech is feeding and push the sucker away sideways.

When the seal made by the oral sucker is broken, the leech will stop feeding. After the oral sucker has been dislodged, the leech's head will seek to reattach, and it may quickly attach to the finger that displaced the head. Even if the oral sucker attaches again, the leech does not begin to feed immediately.

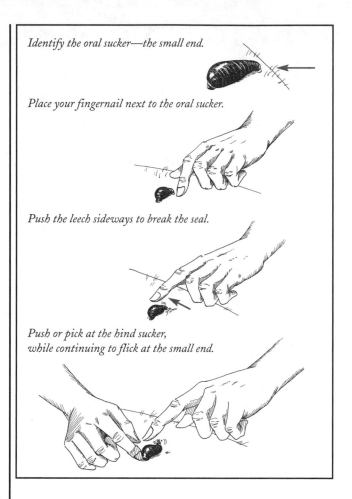

Identify the oral sucker—the small end.

Place your fingernail next to the oral sucker.

Push the leech sideways to break the seal.

*Push or pick at the hind sucker,
while continuing to flick at the small end.*

5 | **Displace the posterior (hind) sucker.**
While continuing to flick occasionally at the small end, push at or pick under the large end (hind sucker) with a fingernail to cause it to lose its suction.

6 Dispose of the leech.
At this point, the leech may have securely attached itself to the finger you used to remove it. Flick it off—it should detach easily. Once the leech is detached, you can put salt or insect repellent directly on it to keep it from attaching to anything else.

7 Treat the wound.
After the leech's anticoagulants lose their effect, the wound should heal quickly. Keep the area clean, and cover it with a small bandage if necessary. Avoid scratching the wound. If itching becomes severe, take an antihistamine.

IF A LEECH INVADES AN AIR PASSAGE

Hirudiniasis is a potentially serious condition in which one or more leeches invade a body orifice. In particular, *Dinobdella ferox* (literally, "the terrifying ferocious leech" or "nasal leech") has a predilection for airways, where it may cause a blockage or asphyxiation, especially if leeches invade the passage in large numbers. If there is a leech invading your airway and you can breathe, do not attempt to remove it—seek medical attention immediately. If you cannot breathe, take the following steps:

1 Gargle with diluted 80-proof alcohol.
Most distilled liquors—vodka, gin, bourbon, scotch—have the requisite alcohol content. Use a mixture of 50 percent alcohol, 50 percent water. Be careful not to aspirate (inhaling the leech and the alcohol).

how to remove a leech

2 Spit out the leech.

Alternative
If gargling does not work and the leech is visible, remove it by grasping firmly at the hind sucker and yanking.

Be Aware
- There is virtually no risk of substantial blood loss from leech bites. The wound will continue to bleed for some time after a leech has finished feeding, but this level of blood loss is not dangerous.
- Leeches are generally not known to transmit blood parasites to humans.
- Leeches are more likely to be encountered in still water than in rivers or streams. They are more often found near the edges of clean, clear water than in or near swamps.
- Leeches need a solid surface to hold on to even when they are not feeding. Avoid leeches by staying in the open: Swim in deep, open water, avoid boat docks, and do not wade through areas with submerged branches or rocks. In jungles, remain on trails and be aware of leeches on overhanging branches and vines.
- Both aquatic and terrestrial leeches have incredible senses of perception. They are attracted by vibrations and by body heat, and they have 10 pairs of eyes to detect movement. Keep moving, and check yourself and your traveling companions regularly.

HOW TO TREAT A SCORPION STING

1 Remain calm.
Scorpion venom induces anxiety in victims, so try especially hard to avoid panic. Most species of scorpion have venom of low to moderate toxicity and do not pose a serious health threat to adult humans, other than severe pain.

2 Apply heat or cold packs to the sting site for pain relief.
The most severe pain usually occurs at the site of the sting. Also use an analgesic (painkiller) if available.

3 If an allergic reaction occurs, take an antihistamine.
Scorpion venom contains histamines, which may cause allergic reactions (asthma, rashes) in sensitive persons.

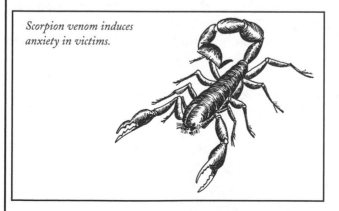

Scorpion venom induces anxiety in victims.

4 Watch for an irregular heartbeat, tingling in extremities, an inability to move limbs or fingers, or trouble breathing.

Most scorpion stings cause only instantaneous pain at the site of the sting; stings feel similar to those of a wasp. The pain of a scorpion sting may radiate over the body several minutes after the initial sting. Pain tends to be felt in joints, especially in the armpits and groin. Systemic symptoms may also occur—possibly numbness in the face, mouth, or throat; muscle twitches; sweating; nausea; vomiting; fever; and restlessness. These symptoms are normal and not life-threatening, and usually subside in one to three hours. The site of the sting may remain sore and/or sensitive to touch, heat, or cold for one to three days.

5 Seek emergency medical care if you exhibit the above symptoms.

Small children who are stung should seek emergency medical care immediately. Adults, however, have much more time—the odds of dying or even becoming seriously ill as a result of a scorpion sting are extremely slim. You will have at least 12 hours to get to a hospital—probably more.

6 Do not apply tourniquets, as the toxins are small and move extremely rapidly away from the site of the sting.

A tourniquet will not help the wound, and could cause more harm if applied incorrectly.

7 | Do not attempt to cut the wound and suck out the poison.

This can cause infection or transfer the venom into the bloodstream of the person attempting to remove the poison.

Be Aware

- Scorpions are active at night, when they hunt and search for mates. During the day, scorpions hide in burrows or in any available crack or crevice, depending upon the species. Scorpions are notorious for seeking shelter in objects such as shoes, clothing, bedding, and bath towels. Your presence may surprise the scorpion and it could sting if disturbed. If you are in an area that has scorpions, shake out these items before using them, and check bedding before sleeping.

- Many species of scorpions will readily enter homes and other buildings, which increases the likelihood of an encounter. Scorpions will sting if surprised or threatened, but generally will not sting if unprovoked.

- Scorpions cannot usually deliver enough venom to kill a healthy adult. While venom toxicity varies among species, some scorpions contain very powerful neurotoxins, which, ounce for ounce, are more toxic to humans than the venom of cobras. However, scorpions inject relatively small amounts of venom (compared to snakes), so the overall dose of toxins per sting is survivable.

HOW TO CROSS A PIRANHA-INFESTED RIVER

1 Do not cross if you have an open wound.
Piranhas are attracted to blood.

2 Avoid areas with netted fish, docks where fish are
cleaned, and areas around bird rookeries.
Piranhas may become habituated to feeding in these
areas and may be more aggressive there.

3 Stay out of the water when piranhas are feeding.
When large numbers of piranhas are attacking prey—
a true feeding frenzy—they may snap and bite at
anything around them. If you see them feeding, stay
away, or well upriver.

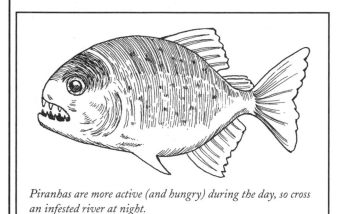

*Piranhas are more active (and hungry) during the day, so cross
an infested river at night.*

4 | Cross the river at night.
Virtually every species of piranha rests at night, and when awakened, will swim away rather than attack. Piranhas are most active at dawn, though some large adults may hunt in the evening.

5 | Swim or walk across quickly and quietly.
Try not to create a large disturbance in the water that might awaken piranhas.

Be Aware

- Piranhas are freshwater, tropical fish. In the wild, they exist only in South America, in slow-moving rivers, backwaters, or floodplain lakes. Piranhas generally do not live in either mountain lakes or streams; the water is too cold and flows too fast.
- Piranhas generally do not attack humans or large animals—unless they are already dead or injured. During the dry season, however, when their food supply is scarce, piranhas can be more aggressive. When driving cattle across a river suspected of containing piranhas, farmers will sometimes sacrifice a sick or injured animal downstream before letting the herd enter the water.

HOW TO SPOT A
RABID ANIMAL

1 Watch out for raccoons, skunks, and bats.
All warm-blooded animals can carry rabies, but the disease is most common among these animals. Coyotes, foxes, and larger rodents, such as groundhogs, can also carry rabies. It is rare among mice, squirrels, chipmunks, guinea pigs, hamsters, rabbits, rats, and other small rodents.

2 If the animal is foaming or appears to have a locked jaw, stay away.
There are two type of rabies: "furious" rabies and "dumb" rabies. Animals with the former are hostile, may snap and bite, and have an increase in saliva, which makes their mouths appear to be foaming. Animals with the latter (also called paralytic rabies) are timid and shy, and may have paralysis of the lower jaw and muscles.

3 If you are bitten by any animal, immediately wash the bite out with soap and running warm water.
The wound can also be treated with an antiseptic such as hydrogen peroxide or an antibiotic ointment. Dress the wound with a sterile cloth or bandage, and put pressure on the wound to stop bleeding. Get professional medical attention as soon as possible.

4 Call animal control authorities to report the incident. Describe the animal and where you were when you received the bite so that they can try to catch the animal. Tests will determine if the animal has rabies. Without the animal to test, the medical treatment may mean painful injections, since health providers will have to assume the animal had rabies. Do not try to catch the animal yourself.

5 Monitor your health.
Early symptoms of rabies include mental depression, restlessness, and abnormal sensations such as itching around the site of the bite, headache, fever, tiredness, nausea, sore throat, or loss of appetite. Other early symptoms include muscle stiffness, dilation of pupils, increased production of saliva, and unusual sensitivity to sound, light, and changes of temperature. Symptoms usually develop within two to eight weeks after infection. The more severe the bite, the sooner the onset of symptoms.

Be Aware
Generally, you will know if a wild animal has bitten you. However, bat bites can be small and may not be felt. A bat that is active by day, that is found in a place where bats are not usually seen, or that is unable to fly is far more likely to be rabid.

CHAPTER 2
GREAT ESCAPES

HOW TO JUMP FROM ROOFTOP TO ROOFTOP

1   **Look for any obstructions if you have time.**
You may have to clear short walls, gutters, or other obstacles as well as the space between buildings.

2   **Check your target building.**
Make certain that you have enough space to land and roll. If the target building is lower than your building, assess how much lower it is. You risk broken ankles or legs if there is more than a one-story differential in the buildings. If there are two stories or more, you risk a broken back.

3   **Check the distance between the buildings.**
Most people cannot jump farther than 10 feet, even at a full run. If the buildings are farther apart than this distance, you risk catastrophic injury or death. You must clear the distance and land on the other roof, or be able to grab on to a ledge on the other side. If the target building is lower, your forward momentum will continue to carry you even as you fall, so you may be able to leap a greater distance—though probably not more than about 12 feet. You could successfully leap a span across an alley, but not a two-lane road.

Jump with your arms outstretched, ready to grab the ledge if you undershoot your mark.

4 Pick a spot for take off and a spot for landing.

5 Run at full speed toward the edge.
You must be running as fast as possible to attempt a leap of a distance of more than a few feet. You will need 40 to 60 feet of running room to develop enough speed to clear about 10 feet.

6 Leap.

Make sure your center of gravity is over the edge of your target building in case your whole body doesn't clear the span and you have to grab hold. Jump with your arms and hands extended and ready to grab the ledge.

7 Try to land on your feet, then immediately tuck your head and tumble sideways onto your shoulders, not forward onto your head.

Because you will not be moving fast, it is safe to roll head over heels, unlike jumping from a moving vehicle.

HOW TO
JUMP FROM A
BUILDING INTO
A DUMPSTER

1 Jump straight down.
If you leap off and away from the building at an angle, your trajectory will make you miss the Dumpster. Resist your natural tendency to push off.

2 Tuck your head and bring your legs around.
To do this during the fall, execute a three-quarter revolution—basically, a not-quite-full somersault. This is the only method that will allow a proper landing, with your back facing down.

3 Aim for the center of the Dumpster or large box of debris.

4 Land flat on your back so that when your body folds, your feet and hands meet.
When your body hits any surface from a significant height, the body folds into a V. This means landing on your stomach can result in a broken back.

1. *Jump straight down.*

2. *Tuck your head and bring your legs around, executing a three-quarter somersault.*

3. *Aim for the center of the Dumpster and land flat on your back.*

Be Aware

- If the building has fire escapes or other protrusions, your leap will have to be far enough out so you miss them on your way down. The landing target needs to be far enough from the building for you to hit it.

- The Dumpster may be filled with bricks or other unfriendly materials. It is entirely possible to survive a high fall (five stories or more) into a Dumpster, provided it is filled with the right type of trash (cardboard boxes are best) and you land correctly.

HOW TO JUMP FROM A MOVING TRAIN

1 Move to the end of the last car.
If this is not an option, you can jump from the space between cars, or from the door if you can get it open.

2 If you have time, wait for the train to slow as it rounds a bend in the tracks.
If you jump and land correctly, you will probably survive even at high speeds (70 mph or more), but you increase your chances of survival if the train is moving slowly.

3 Stuff blankets, clothing, or seat cushions underneath your clothes.
Wear a thick or rugged jacket if possible. Use a belt to secure some padding around your head, but make certain you can see clearly. Pad your knees, elbows, and hips.

4 Pick your landing spot before you jump.
The ideal spot will be relatively soft and free of obstructions. Avoid trees, bushes, and, of course, rocks.

5 Get as low to the floor as possible, bending your knees so you can leap away from the train car.

Pick your landing spot, and jump as far away from the train as you can. Protect your head.

Try to land so that all parts of your body hit the ground at the same time.

Roll like a log, keeping your head protected.

6 Jump perpendicular to the train, leaping as far away from the train as you can.

Even if you jump from the last car, leap at right angles to the direction of the train. This way, your momentum will not carry you toward the wheels and tracks.

7 Cover and protect your head with your hands and arms, and roll like a log when you land.

Do not try to land on your feet. Keep your body straight and try to land so that all parts of your body hit the ground at the same time—you will absorb the impact over a wider area. If you land on your feet, you will most likely break your ankles or legs. Do NOT roll head over heels as if doing a forward somersault.

HOW TO JUMP FROM A BRIDGE OR CLIFF INTO A RIVER

When attempting a high fall (over twenty feet) into water in an emergency situation, you will not know much about your surroundings, specifically the depth of the water. This makes jumping particularly dangerous.

If jumping from a bridge into a river or other body of water with boat traffic, try to land in the channel—the deepwater area where boats go under the bridge. This area is generally in the center, away from the shoreline.

Stay away from any area with pylons that are supporting the bridge. Debris can collect in these areas and you can hit it when you enter the water.

Swim to shore immediately after surfacing.

How to Jump

1 Jump feet first.

2 Keep your body completely vertical.

3 Squeeze your feet together.

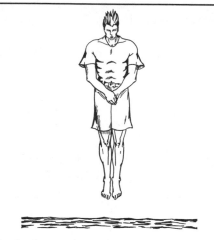

Jump feet first in a vertical position; squeeze your feet together; clench your backside and protect your crotch.

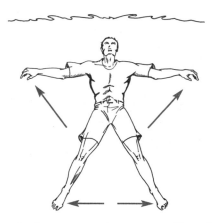

After you enter the water, spread your arms and legs wide and move them back and forth, which will slow your plunge. Attempt to slow your descent.

4 | Enter the water feet first, and clench your buttocks together.
If you do not, water may rush in and cause severe internal damage.

5 | Protect your crotch area by covering it with your hands.

6 | Immediately after you hit the water, spread your arms and legs wide and move them back and forth to generate resistance, which will slow your plunge to the bottom.
Always assume the water is not deep enough to keep you from hitting bottom.

Be Aware

- Hitting the water as described above could save your life, although it may break your legs.
- If your body is not straight, you can break your back upon entry. Keep yourself vertical until you hit the water.
- Do not even think about going in headfirst unless you are absolutely sure that the water is at least twenty feet deep. If your legs hit the bottom, they will break. If your head hits, your skull will break.

HOW TO
SURVIVE IF YOUR
PARACHUTE
FAILS TO OPEN

1 As soon as you realize that your chute is bad, signal to a jumping companion whose chute has not yet opened that you are having a malfunction.
Wave your arms and point to your chute.

2 When your companion (and new best friend) gets to you, hook arms.

3 Once you are hooked together, the two of you will still be falling at terminal velocity, or about 130 miles per hour.
When your friend opens his chute, there will be no way either of you will be able hold on to one another normally, because the G-forces will triple or quadruple your body weight. To prepare for this problem, hook your arms into his chest strap, or through the two sides of the front of his harness, all the way up to your elbows, and grab hold of your own strap.

4 Open the chute.
The chute opening shock will be severe, probably enough to dislocate or break your arms.

Hook arms with your companion. Then hook your arms into his chest strap, up to the elbows, and grab hold of your own.

5 Steer the canopy.

Your friend must now hold on to you with one arm while steering his canopy (the part of the chute that controls direction and speed).

If your friend's canopy is slow and big, you may hit the grass or dirt slowly enough to break only a leg, and your chances of survival are high.

If his canopy is a fast one, however, your friend will have to steer to avoid hitting the ground too fast. You must also avoid power lines and other obstructions at all costs.

6 If there is a body of water nearby, head for that. Of course, once you hit the water, you will have to tread with just your legs and hope that your partner is able to pull you out before your chute takes in water.

How to Prepare

Check your chute before you jump. The good news is that today's parachutes are built to open, so even if you make big mistakes packing them, they tend to sort themselves out. The reserve chute, however, must be packed by a certified rigger and must be perfect as it is your last resort. Make sure that:

- The parachute is folded in straight lines—that there are no twists.
- The slider is positioned correctly to keep the parachute from opening too fast.

HOW TO GET
TO THE SURFACE
IF YOUR SCUBA TANK
RUNS OUT OF AIR

1 Do not panic.

2 Signal to your fellow divers that you are having a problem—point to your tank or regulator.

3 If someone comes to your aid, share their regulator, passing it back and forth while swimming slowly to the surface.
Take two breaths, then pass it back to the other diver. Ascend together, exhaling as you go. Then take another two breaths, alternating, until you reach the surface. Nearly all divers carry an extra regulator connected to their tank.

4 If no one can help you, keep your regulator in your mouth; air may expand in the tank as you ascend, giving you additional breaths.

5 Look straight up so that your airway is as straight as possible.

6 Swim to the surface at a slow to moderate rate. Exhale continuously as you swim up. It is very important that you exhale the entire way up, but the rate at

Keep your regulator in your mouth.

Keep your airway as straight as possible by looking toward the surface.

Swim at a slow to moderate rate, exhaling continuously.

how to get to the surface if your scuba tank runs out of air

which you exhale is also important. Exhale slowly—
do not exhaust all your air in the first few seconds of
your ascent. As long as you are even slightly exhaling,
your passageway will be open and air can vent from
your lungs.

WARNING: If you do not exhale continuously, you
risk an embolism.

Be Aware

- Never dive alone.
- Watch your pressure and depth gauges closely.
- Make sure your fellow divers are within easy
  signaling/swimming distance.
- Share a regulator in an emergency. It is much
  safer to use your partner's regulator than to try
  to make a quick swim to the surface. This is
  especially true the deeper you are, where you
  need to surface gradually.
- Always use an alternate air source instead of
  swimming up unless you are fewer than thirty feet
  below the surface.

HOW TO RETRIEVE A CANDY BAR STUCK IN THE LUNCHROOM VENDING MACHINE

1 Wait several seconds.
Newer vending machines may be equipped with special technology that senses when an item has not dropped; the machine may return your money or give you another selection.

2 Purchase the item again.
Depending on how severely the snack is stuck and how much money you have, you may be able to jar it loose and get a second one by selecting the same item again.

3 Choose an item from the row above.
If your snack is stuck at an angle toward the glass at the end of the row, an item dropping from above may knock it free.

4 Jostle the machine.
Vending machines are extremely heavy and can cause major injury if they tip over. Carefully bang on the side of the machine. Do not hit glass areas.

Rock the machine forward and back slightly.

5 **Rock the machine.**
Tip the machine backward very slightly (not side-to-side) and let it drop back in place to jar the item loose. Do not press on the glass.

6 **Push in the vending door and remove the candy.**
Once the item—or items—have dropped, reach in and slowly extricate it.

Be Aware
Anti-theft devices make it virtually impossible to reach in and up past the vending door. Do not risk getting your arm stuck in the machine.

HOW TO FREE YOURSELF
FROM A COAT HOOK

Unbutton your shirt or coat, starting with the top button, just enough to slip out of your garment and slide to the ground. Then unhook your clothes and put them back on. If you were hung by your coat, you just leave it there on the hook.

HOW TO SURVIVE A BORING CLASS

★ **Pull your hair or pinch yourself.**
Making yourself physically uncomfortable will make you less likely to fall asleep.

★ **Wear as few items of clothing as possible.**
The cold will keep you awake.

★ **Hide more interesting reading material.**
Prop open your textbook and conceal a novel or magazine inside it. Hold a highlighter in your hand and pretend to be taking notes as you read.

★ **Suggest holding class outside.**
If the weather is nice, ask the professor to teach out on the college green. This strategy rarely works for large survey classes or the sciences.

★ **Send text messages on your cell phone.**
Engage in a running text message exchange with other students in the class about how bad the professor is. Make sure that your keypad is set to mute so that you do not distract other students around you or draw your professor's attention to yourself.

★ **Make paper airplanes.**
Make as many models as you can. Pretend they are having fierce battles.

Paper Airplane

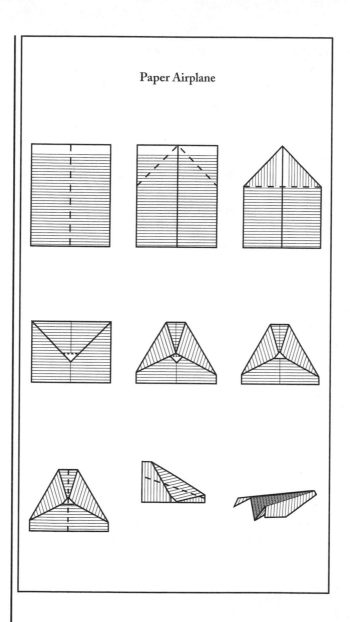

★ | Keep a list of words with dirty meanings.
Write down words with alternate sexual meanings *(melons, stock, position, score)* as they are spoken by your professor. In the right frame of mind, almost any word will work.

★ | Take notes with your nondominant hand.
Concentrate on staying in the lines.

★ | Take notes in a foreign language.
Practice your language skills by translating your professor's lecture. Bring along your translation dictionary to increase your vocabulary.

★ | Keep a superlative log.
Identify the most interesting people in the class on a daily basis. Observe how people change over time. Categories could include:
- Most attractive
- Tallest
- Blondest
- Ugliest
- Dirtiest
- Dumbest

★ | Pretend you are a secret agent.
You are on a dangerous mission and must make it through the class alive. Spy on people to see what they are writing. Use a small hand mirror and a penlight to send Morse code to a confederate across the room.

How to Sleep in Class

1 | **Wear a hat.**
Sharply bend the brim of a baseball cap and pull the visor low over your face to hide your eyes in the shadow. Do not wear a wool ski hat, beanie, or yarmulke, as none of these casts a shadow.

2 | **Sit in the rear of the class.**
Choose a seat in the back of the classroom or at least far enough from your professor that he will not notice your heavy breathing.

in back   lying down (wrong)   head on desk (wrong)   hat   hidden   napping position   slumped (wrong)

3 | Sit behind a tall person.
Position yourself behind a member of the basketball or volleyball team to interrupt your professor's line of vision. Sitting behind an obese person can also block your professor's sight line.

4 | Sit on the opposite side of the class from known class participants.

5 | Pad the desktop in front of you.
Fold a scarf, sweater, or sweatshirt on your desk. Bend one arm and place your elbow on the folded item.

6 | Assume the napping position.
- Place your thumb under your chin, supporting your jaw.
- Rest your four fingers on the side of your face.
- Balance your head on your hand, keeping it upright.
- Place your notebook open and in front of you; hold a pen in your other hand, to look as if you are ready to take notes.

Be Aware
- Avoid wearing dark sunglasses in class. While they may serve to shade your eyes, they also attract attention.
- Do not let your head slump down to your chest.
- Do not rest your head on your desk.
- Do not lie down.

How to Survive If Caught Passing a Note in Class

Swallow the note immediately. Do not give the teacher a chance to grab it and read it out loud. You are already in trouble for passing a note—there is no point in adding the humiliation of having it read to the class.

HOW TO HIDE THINGS IN YOUR DORM ROOM

SMALL ITEM

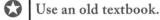 **Use an old textbook.**
Stash cash between pages. For other items, make a secret compartment.
- Open the book to page 50 or beyond.
- Use a razor blade or a sharp knife to cut a square hole in the center of the book. Use a metal ruler to guide you, and keep repeating your cut lines to go deeper and deeper.
- Remove the square cut-out pages.
- Put the item in the compartment.
- Reshelve the book.

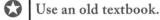 **Use a potted plant.**
- Seal the item in a plastic bag.
- Dig a hole several inches deep in the soil.
- Bury the bag.

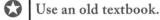 **Construct a beer can safe.**
- Using a nail or pen, poke a small hole in one side of a beer can, near the bottom. Drink or discard the contents.
- Use scissors or tin snips to cut away the side of the can with the hole, leaving the top and bottom intact.

Select a thick book.

Cut vertically.

Cut horizontally.

Remove pages.

- Stash valuables in the can and place it on a wall covered with other, similar cans. Make sure the hole in the can faces the wall.

⭐ **Use electrical outlets.**
This location is suitable for very small and dry items only.
- Use a screwdriver to unscrew the switch plate that surrounds a light switch or electrical outlet.
- Insert the item in the wall cavity.
- Replace the plate.

⭐ **Use shampoo bottles.**
- Seal the item in a waterproof bag.
- Hide the bag in a bottle of shampoo.
- Keep your bathroom items separate from your roommate's to avoid detection.

⭐ **Use baseboards.**
- Pry a small section of baseboard away from the wall, using a hammer and chisel or flat screwdriver.
- Use the hammer to pound a hole in the drywall just above the floor, in an area that will be concealed by the baseboard.
- Stash the item in the hole.
- Replace the baseboard by wedging it in place.

Large Item

★ Camouflage.
Pile dirty or damp clothing on the item to be hidden. Make sure the pile looks and smells sufficiently unappealing to prevent scrutiny.

★ Use a feather pillow.
Depending on the size and weight of the item, you may be able to stash it in a feather pillow. Unzip the pillow and bury the item in the middle. Make sure all hard edges are well covered with several inches of feathers. Re-zip and cover with a dirty pillowcase to deter inspection.

★ Use your roommate.
If you suspect you will be the subject of a search (particularly a search by a thieving roommate), hide valuables among your roommate's possessions. Make sure the hidden item is well concealed in the back of a closet, under her bed, or in another location she is unlikely to visit regularly. Check periodically to be certain the hidden item has not been detected.

How to Survive a Shattered/ Colapsing Basketball Backboard

Step past the end line behind the backboard—the structure will come forward if torn off its moorings. Bend toward the floor and cover the back of your head with your hands.

HOW TO SURVIVE
A FALL ONTO
SUBWAY TRACKS

1 Do not attempt to climb back onto the platform
unless you are certain that you have enough time
to do so.
If a train is approaching, you will need to act quickly.

2 Avoid areas of the ground near the track and the wall
that are marked with a strip of tape or with red and
white painted stripes.
Such markings indicate that the train passes extremely
close to these areas, and you will not have enough clearance. In areas with these markings, there should be
alcoves every several yards. These alcoves are safe to
stand in if you can fit within them.

3 If the tracks are near a wall, check to see if there
is enough space to stand between the train and
the wall.
Clearance of $1\frac{1}{2}$ to 2 feet should be enough. Remove
any articles of clothing or bags that could catch on the
train. Stand straight, still, and tall facing the train,
which will pass just inches in front of you.

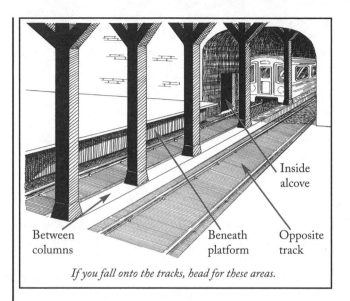

If you fall onto the tracks, head for these areas.

Inside
alcove

Between
columns

Beneath
platform

Opposite
track

4 If the tracks are located between the platform and another set of tracks, you may be able to move to the other track instead.

Be mindful of trains approaching on the other side. Cross the third rail (which carries the electric current) by stepping completely over it—do not step on the wooden guard, since it may not hold you.

5 If a line of columns separates the tracks from other tracks, stand between the columns.

Remove any articles of clothing or bags that could catch on the train, and stand straight, still, and tall.

6 Check to see if there is enough space for you to crawl under the lip of the concrete platform and avoid the train.

Use this only as a last resort—this strategy is not recommended since all platforms are different.

Alternatives

If none of these options is feasible, you have two other choices.

• Run past the leading end of the platform, beyond where the front car will stop.

 Since trains running on the track closest to the platform are likely to stop at a station (as opposed to express trains, which usually run on center tracks), you can clear the train by running well past the leading end of the platform and thus the front car. (Note: This method will not work for express trains that only stop at some stations, so you are taking your chances.)

• If there is a depression in the concrete between the rails, lie down into it—there will be enough room for a train to pass over you. (Use this method only in desperation—the train may be dragging something, or there may not be enough clearance.)

How to Survive Being Car-Doored on a Bicycle

Throw your weight backward. Stand on the pedals and above the seat. Apply only the rear brakes. Turn slightly to the side to disperse the impact as you hit the door. If you land in the street, move immediately toward the curb to get out of the way of traffic.

HOW TO SURVIVE
A HIGH-RISE
HOTEL FIRE

Always treat a hotel fire alarm seriously, and exit following hotel procedure. If the fire is nearby, use the following procedure.

1 **Feel your hotel room doorknob with the back of your hand.**
If the doorknob is hot to the touch, go to step 2 and then skip to step 5. If it is not hot, follow the steps in order.

2 **Partially fill the bathtub with cold water.**
Soak towels, washcloths, bedsheets, and blankets in the water. If the water is off, use water from the toilet tank. Put a wet washcloth over your mouth and nose and a wet sheet or towel over your head.

3 **Open the door.**

4 **If the hallway is smoke-filled, get as low as possible—one to two feet above the floor.**
Make your way to an emergency exit. Never use the elevator.

5 If the door or doorknob is hot, do not open the door.
Wedge wet towels in the crack under the door to keep smoke out.

6 Try calling the front desk or rooms on other floors to check on conditions in other areas.

If you cannot escape through the door, make a tent of wet towels or sheets at an open window to protect you from smoke and to allow you to breathe outside air.

7 | Turn off fans and air conditioners that could draw smoke into the room, and open the window slightly. If the fire is on a floor below you, smoke may enter the room through the window, so keep the opening narrow. If the fire is not below you, open the window a third or halfway.

8 | Make a tent of wet towels and sheets at the window. Do not build the tent if smoke is billowing into the room. Hold or attach one side of the towel or sheet to the window and allow the other side to fall behind you, so you are protected from smoke and are breathing outside air. The towels should help to cool the air and make it easier to breathe.

9 | Signal rescue personnel with a white towel or a flashlight.
Wait for rescue.

10 | If the air in the room is getting worse, breathing becomes difficult, and no rescue is forthcoming, try to kick through the wall into the adjacent room. Closets are the best locations to try to break through. Sit on the floor of the closet, and knock on the wall until you hear a hollow sound. (Wall studs are normally spaced 16 inches apart.) Use both feet to kick through both surfaces of drywall. You may survive by using this as a breathing hole, or you may need to continue breaching the wall until you can escape into the next room.

11 If you cannot breach the wall, go to a window and look at the outside of the building.

If the rooms have balconies that are close together, consider climbing to another balcony on the same floor. If there are no neighboring balconies, you can tie bedsheets together and climb to a balcony directly beneath yours. Use square knots (the first step in tying your shoes, done twice) and lower yourself one floor only. Consider this option only as a last resort, and only do it if you are attempting to escape an immediate danger or to reach rescue personnel.

Be Aware

- Ladders on fire trucks usually reach only to the seventh floor of a high-rise building. Consider booking a room below this level.
- Poolside or courtyard rooms are likely to be inaccessible to ladder trucks, even if they are below the seventh floor. Consider staying in a streetside room.
- Upon check-in, make sure the hotel has smoke detectors and fire sprinklers.
- Count the doors between your room and the nearest fire exit. This will help you get out safely if smoke reduces visibility.
- Keep your room key where it can be found in the dark.
- Never jump from a height of more than two floors or you risk death.

HOW TO BREAK DOWN A DOOR

Interior Doors

1 Give the door a well-placed kick or two to the lock area to break it down.

Running at the door and slamming against it with your shoulder or body is not usually as effective as kicking with your foot. Your foot exerts more force than your shoulder, and you will be able to direct this force toward the area of the locking mechanism more succinctly with your foot.

Alternate Method
(if you have a screwdriver)

⭐ Look on the front of the doorknob for a small hole or keyhole.

Most interior doors have what are called privacy sets. These locks are usually installed on bedrooms and bathrooms and can be locked from the inside when the door is shut, but have an emergency access hole in the center of the door handle which allows entry to the locking mechanism inside. Insert the screwdriver or probe into the handle and push the locking mechanism, or turn the mechanism to open the lock.

Exterior Doors

If you are trying to break down an exterior door, you will need more force. Exterior doors are of sturdier construction and are designed with security in mind, for obvious reasons. In general, you can expect to see two kinds of latches on outside doors: a passage- or entry-lock set for latching and a dead-bolt lock for security. The passage set is used for keeping the door from swinging open and does not lock. The entry-lock set utilizes a dead latch and can be locked before closing the door.

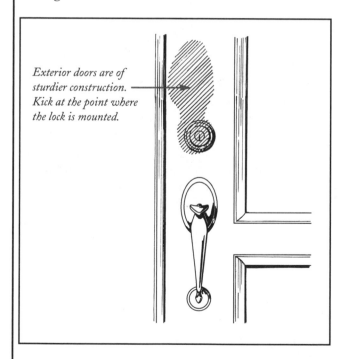

Exterior doors are of sturdier construction. Kick at the point where the lock is mounted.

1 Give the door several well-placed kicks at the point where the lock is mounted.

An exterior door usually takes several tries to break down this way, so keep at it.

Alternate Method
(if you have a sturdy piece of steel)

⭐ Wrench or pry the lock off the door by inserting the tool between the lock and the door and prying back and forth.

Alternate Method
(if you have a screwdriver, hammer, and awl)

⭐ Remove the pins from the hinges (if the door opens toward you) and then force the door open from the hinge side.

Get a screwdriver or an awl and a hammer. Place the awl or screwdriver underneath the hinge, with the pointy end touching the end of the bolt or screw. Using the hammer, strike the other end of the awl or screwdriver until the hinge comes out.

ASSESSING AMOUNT OF FORCE REQUIRED

Interior doors in general are of a lighter construction than exterior doors and usually are thinner—1$\frac{3}{8}$" thick to 1$\frac{5}{8}$" thick—than exterior doors, which generally are 1$\frac{3}{4}$" thick. In general, older homes will be more likely to have solid wood doors, while newer ones will have the cheaper, hollow core models. Knowing what type of door you are dealing with will

how to break down a door

help you determine how to break it down. You can usually determine the construction and solidity of a door by tapping on it.

HOLLOW CORE. This type is generally used for interior doors, since it provides no insulation or security, and requires minimal force. These doors can often be opened with a screwdriver.

SOLID WOOD. These are usually oak or some other hardwood, and require an average amount of force and a crowbar or other similar tool.

SOLID CORE. These have a softwood inner frame with a laminate on each side and a chipped or shaved wood core, and require an average amount of force and a screwdriver.

METAL CLAD. These are usually softwood with a thin metal covering, and require average or above-average force and a crowbar.

HOLLOW METAL. These doors are of a heavier-gauge metal that usually has a reinforcing channel around the edges and the lock mounting area, and are sometimes filled with some type of insulating material. These require maximum force and a crowbar.

HOW TO EVADE A STAMPEDE OF SHOPPERS

 Stay focused and visualize your goal.

Do not freeze in front of the pack; do not wait for the crowd of shoppers to get close before you make your move. Reacting early and decisively in crowds offers your best shot at survival.

Brace for an oncoming crowd by wrapping your arms tightly around your packages.

★ **Avoid herd mentality.**
Animals travel in herds because there is safety in numbers, and the safest place is at the center of the pack, insulated from predators. Avoid the temptation to join the herd—you cannot shop if you cannot see the merchandise.

★ **Do not move toward the oncoming herd.**
You risk being trampled if you try to thread your way through a stampede. If you are unable to get out of the way of a fast-moving crowd, bring your arms in tightly around any packages you are carrying, turn your body in the direction of the crowd, and let yourself be carried along as you work your way to the outside of the herd.

★ **Maximize your movement options.**
If you need to negotiate a crowd, stay on the edge. Use the space near the walls to gain a few extra yards of room. Most shoppers will leave at least several feet between themselves and surrounding walls. This will give you room to maneuver.

Be Aware
When heading into a shopping situation where crowds may be present, wear proper shoes. Open-toed shoes offer minimal protection for your feet, and high heels will restrict your mobility. Select shoes with flat heels. Rubber soles provide better traction.

How to Penetrate a Crowd to Get the Last Item on the Shelf

1 | Move slowly and decisively toward the front without appearing too aggressive.
Shoving or cutting people off will provoke flying elbows and closed ranks.

2 | Keep your eyes on the other shoppers, so you can anticipate their movements.

3 | Maintain a calm demeanor as you close in on the target item.
Breathe evenly and slowly. Avoid signaling your urgency, which might alert the crowd to the desirability of the toy or other target. Avoid stepping on toes or panicking other shoppers, which may cause a stampede.

4 | Smile.

5 | Grab the item.
Tuck it under your arm as you would a football to prevent it from being knocked or torn loose.

6 | Proceed to the nearest cash register.
Continue to move with the crowd until you are able to slip down an aisle unnoticed.

how to evade a stampede of shoppers

How to Escape from a Collapsed Sofa Bed

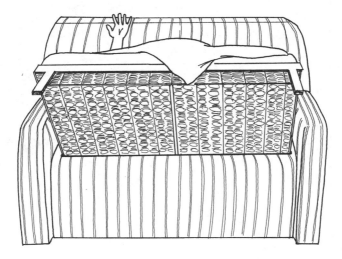

Grasp the top edge of the bed if your arms are free and pull your lower body away from the folding section. If your arms are pinned, dig your heels into the mattress and push to lift the folding section enough to shift position. Wriggle to the edge of the bed, grasp a sofa arm, and pull yourself free.

HOW TO FREE
YOUR LEG FROM
A BEAR TRAP

1 | Move your foot and wiggle your toes.
Bear traps are designed to catch and hold the leg of a bear, not cut it off. Your leg may be badly bruised, but it should not be severely injured or amputated. Attempt to move your foot and toes to determine if you still have circulation and to check for tendon and muscle damage. In general, the steel "jaws" of the trap are not sharp. Each side of the jaw should have "teeth" that are designed to allow circulation. If you cannot feel your foot or do not have range of movement, you will have to work quickly.

2 | Sit with the trap in front of you.
Sit on the ground and move the trapped leg so it is in front of you, bent slightly. The trap may be anchored to the ground with a short chain, or the chain may be attached to a loose hook. (When the caught animal runs away, the hook leaves a trail that is easy to track.)

3 | Familiarize yourself with the trap.
The trap will have one piece of bent steel (a "spring") to the left and another piece to the right of the jaws. The center of the trap will have a flat steel plate called a "pan." Your leg will be between the jaws, your foot on the pan.

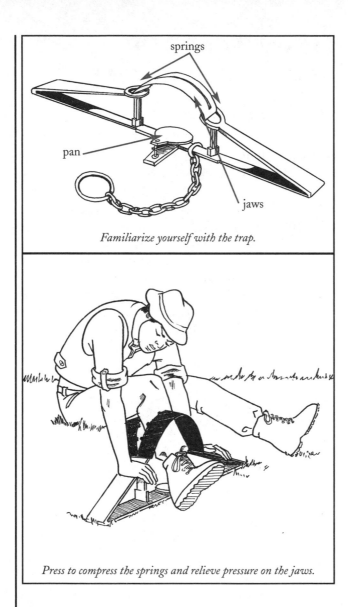

Familiarize yourself with the trap.

Press to compress the springs and relieve pressure on the jaws.

4 Place one hand on the top of each spring.

5 Close the springs.
With as much force as possible, press down hard on the springs to compress them. As the springs compress, they will lower and relieve pressure on the jaws.

6 Once the jaws are loose, slip your foot out of the trap.

7 Release the springs.
Take pressure off the springs slowly to avoid snapping the jaws closed suddenly.

8 Check your leg for damage.
Look for broken skin and tissue damage. Seek medical attention if you are injured. Be sure to request a tetanus booster if metal has pierced the skin.

HOW TO ESCAPE FROM A CAR HANGING OVER THE EDGE OF A CLIFF

1 Do not shift your weight or make any sudden movements.

2 Determine how much time you have.
If the car is like the majority of cars, it is front-wheel drive with the engine in front. This means the bulk of its weight is over the front axle. If the rear, rather than the front, is hanging over the edge of the cliff, you probably have more time to climb out. If the front of the car is over the edge, assess your situation. What is the angle of the car? Is it teetering? Does it sway when you shift your weight? If the car is shifting, you must act quickly.

3 If the front doors are still over land, use these doors to make your escape, regardless of which way your car is facing.
Open the door gradually, move slowly, and get out.

4 If the front doors are over the edge, move to the rear of the car.
Proceed slowly and deliberately; do not jump or lurch. If you have a steering wheel lock or a screwdriver, take it with you—you may need it to get out.

If the front doors are over the edge of the cliff, move slowly to the rear of the car and get out.

how to escape from a car hanging over the edge of a cliff

5 Reassess your situation.

Will opening the rear doors cause the car to slide? If not, open them slowly and get out quickly.

6 **If you think that opening the rear doors will cause the car to slide over the edge, you must break the window.**

Without shifting your weight or rocking the car, use the steering wheel lock or screwdriver to shatter the rear door window (this is safer than breaking the back window because it will require less movement as you climb out). Punch it in the center—the window is made of safety glass and will not injure you.

7 Get out as quickly as possible.

Be Aware

- In situations involving several people, everyone in the front (or everyone in the back) should execute each step simultaneously.
- If driver and passengers are in both front and rear seats, the people who are closest to the edge of the cliff should attempt to get out of the car first.

HOW TO STOP A CAR WITH NO BRAKES

1 Begin pumping the brake pedal and keep pumping it.
You may be able to build up enough pressure in the braking system to slow down a bit, or even stop completely. If you have anti-lock brakes, you do not normally pump them—but if your brakes have failed, this may work.

2 Do not panic—relax and steer the car smoothly.
Cars will often safely corner at speeds much higher than you realize or are used to driving. The rear of the car may slip; steer evenly, being careful not to over-correct.

3 Shift the car into the lowest gear possible and let the engine and transmission slow you down.

4 Pull the emergency brake—but not too hard.
Pulling too hard on the emergency brake will cause the rear wheels to lock, and the car to spin around. Use even, constant pressure. In most cars, the emergency brake (also known as the hand brake or parking brake) is cable operated and serves as a fail-safe brake that should still work even when the rest of the braking system has failed. The car should slow down and, in combination with the lower gear, will eventually stop.

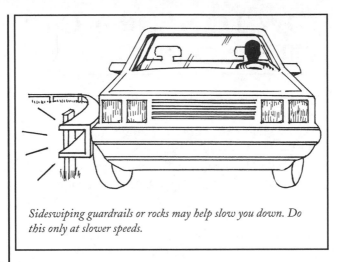

Sideswiping guardrails or rocks may help slow you down. Do this only at slower speeds.

5 If you are running out of room, try a "bootlegger's turn."

Yank the emergency brake hard while turning the wheel a quarter turn in either direction—whichever is safer. This will make the car spin 180 degrees. If you were heading downhill, this spin will head you back uphill, allowing you to slow down.

6 If you have room, swerve the car back and forth across the road.

Making hard turns at each side of the road will decrease your speed even more.

7 If you come up behind another car, use it to help you stop.

Blow your horn, flash your lights, and try to get the driver's attention. If you hit the car, be sure to hit it square, bumper to bumper, so you do not knock the other car off the road. This is an extremely dangerous maneuver: It works best if the vehicle in front of you is larger than yours—a bus or truck is ideal—and if both vehicles are traveling at similar speeds. You do not want to crash into a much slower-moving or stopped vehicle, however.

8 Look for something to help stop you.

A flat or uphill road that intersects with the road you are on, a field, or a fence will slow you further but not stop you suddenly. Scraping the side of your car against a guardrail is another option. Avoid trees and wooden telephone poles: They do not yield as readily.

9 Do not attempt to sideswipe oncoming cars.

10 If none of the above steps has enabled you to stop and you are about to go over a cliff, try to hit something that will slow you down before you go over.

This strategy will also leave a clue to others that someone has gone over the edge. But since very few cliffs are sheer drops, you may fall just several feet and then stop.

HOW TO STOP A
RUNAWAY GOLF CART

If You Are in the Cart

1 Attempt to shut off the cart.
If the cart is electric, turn the ignition key to the "off"
position. If the cart is gas-powered, do not turn the
key to the "off" position—leave it in gear.

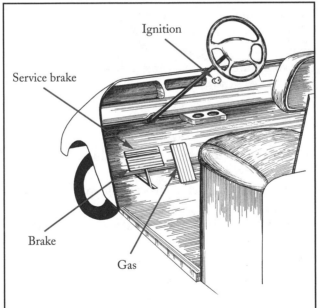

Ignition

Service brake

Brake

Gas

*Push the service, or hill, brake until it sticks. The cart should stop
quickly.*

2 | Try to engage the service brake.
The service, or hill, brake is located on the top half of the brake pedal. Push it forward until it sticks. If it engages, the cart should stop quickly.

3 | If the service brake fails, wait for the automatic emergency system to stop the cart.
If you are still moving, there has been a brake failure. Most late-model electric carts also have "downhill braking," an automatic emergency system that is designed to stop the cart in the event of downhill acceleration. This emergency brake should now engage. Gas carts do not use downhill braking: They have compression braking, which uses the engine to stop the cart experiencing uncontrolled acceleration. This emergency system should also activate automatically.

4 | If the cart does not stop, attempt to ride it out.
You should be able to steer a golf cart even with the key turned off. Stay in the cart and steer onto a gentle incline, which will slow or stop it. Do not jerk the wheel or make any sharp turns. If the car is accelerating downhill or into unsafe terrain and you cannot slow it down, prepare to exit.

5 | Jump out of the cart.
Do not try to land on your feet. Leap out and away from the path of the cart, rolling on your side to lessen the impact until you are at a safe distance. Protect your head with your arms and aim for grass or other forgiving terrain.

Leap out and away from the path of the cart, rolling onto your shoulder. Do not try to land on your feet.

IF YOU ARE NOT IN THE CART

1 Evaluate the situation.

If an empty cart is accelerating downhill and you are far behind, you may not be able to reach it. If the cart is headed uphill or into scrub brush rather than a water hazard, and there are no people in front of the cart, it may slow down on its own. If the cart is headed toward people, a green, or another area where it may cause damage, you may be able to intercept it.

2 Chase the cart and match its speed.

Unless the cart is traveling in a straight line downhill from your position, run at an angle that will allow you to catch up with it.

3 Grab the roof or a roof support.
If the cart is a model without a roof, grab the back of the seat. Do not reach for the wheel before you are in the cart, or you risk turning the cart into your path and running yourself over.

Grab the back of the seat or support pole, then pull yourself aboard with your arms.

4 Swing your body into the cart.
Do not dive into the cart head first. Pull yourself aboard using your arms. Swing your legs in.

5 Turn the steering wheel gently to obtain control.
Do not jerk it.

6 Steer the cart up a rise or into a sand trap.
The sand should slow it down and eventually stop it.

Be Aware

- The industry maximum speed for both electric and gas golf carts is about 14 miles per hour. (Special vehicles can reach speeds of 18 mph.) A runaway golf cart is usually traveling only with momentum, not with electric or gas power, and should not be traveling at more than a few miles per hour, unless it is going down a hill.
- Always set the hill brake when leaving the cart, whether or not you have stopped on a hill.

Failure to set the brake can lead to a runaway cart.

HOW TO
ESCAPE FROM
A SINKING CAR

1 As soon as you hit the water, open your window.
This is your best chance of escape, because opening
the door will be very difficult given the outside water
pressure. (To be safe, you should drive with the windows and doors slightly open whenever you are near
water or are driving on ice.) Opening the windows
allows water to come in and equalize the pressure.
Once the water pressure inside and outside the car is
equal, you'll be able to open the door.

2 If your power windows won't work or you cannot
roll your windows down all the way, attempt to
break the glass with your foot or shoulder or a heavy
object such as an antitheft steering wheel lock.

3 Get out.
Do not worry about leaving anything behind unless
it is another person. Vehicles with engines in front
will sink at a steep angle. If the water is fifteen feet or
deeper, the vehicle may end up on its roof, upside
down. For this reason, you must get out as soon as
possible, while the car is still afloat. Depending on
the vehicle, floating time will range from a few seconds to a few minutes. The more airtight the car, the
longer it floats. Air in the car will quickly be forced

As soon as you hit the water open your window. Otherwise, the pressure of the water will make it very difficult to escape.

If you were unable to exit before hitting the water, attempt to break a window with your foot or a heavy object.

through the trunk and cab, and an air bubble is unlikely to remain once the car hits bottom. Get out as early as possible.

4 | **If you are unable to open the window or break it, you have one final option.**
Remain calm and do not panic. Wait until the car begins filling with water. When the water reaches your

head, take a deep breath and hold it. Now the pressure should be equalized inside and outside, and you should be able to open the door and swim to the surface.

How to Avoid Breaking Through the Ice

- Cars and light trucks need at least eight inches of clear, solid ice on which to drive safely.
- Driving early or late in the season is not advisable.
- Leaving your car in one place for a long period of time can weaken the ice beneath it, and cars should not be parked—or driven—close together.
- Cross any cracks at right angles, and drive slowly.
- New ice is generally thicker than old ice.
- Direct freezing of lake or stream water is stronger than refreezing, freezing of melting snow, or freezing of water bubbling up through cracks.
- If there is a layer of snow on the ice, beware: a layer of snow insulates the ice, slowing the freezing process, and the snow's weight can decrease the bearing capacity of the ice.
- Ice near the shore is weaker.
- River ice is generally weaker than lake ice.
- River mouths are dangerous, because the ice near them is weaker.
- Carry several large nails in your pocket, and a length of rope. The nails will help you pull yourself out of the ice, and the rope can be thrown to someone on more solid ice, or can be used to help someone else.

HOW TO ESCAPE FROM THE TRUNK OF A CAR

1 If you are in a trunk that has no wall separating the backseats and the trunk, try to get the seats down. Although the release for most seats is inside the passenger compartment, you may be able to fold or force them down from the trunk side. (If not, continue to step 2.)

2 Check for a trunk cable underneath the carpet or upholstery.
Many new cars have a trunk release lever on the floor below the driver's seat. These cars should have a cable that runs from the release lever to the trunk. Look for the cable beneath carpeting or upholstery, or behind a panel of sheet metal. If you locate the cable, pull on it to release the trunk latch. (If not, continue to step 3.)

3 Look for a tool in the trunk.
Many cars have emergency kits inside the trunk, underneath or with the spare tire. These kits may contain a screwdriver, flashlight, or pry bar. Use a screwdriver or pry bar to pry the latch open. You can also pry the corner of the trunk lid up and wave and yell to signal passersby. (If there is no tool, continue to step 4.)

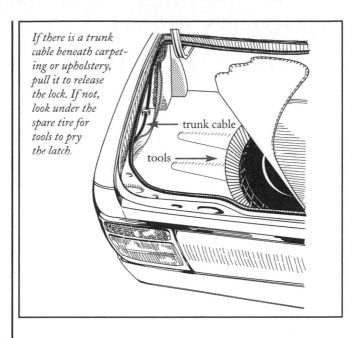

If there is a trunk cable beneath carpeting or upholstery, pull it to release the lock. If not, look under the spare tire for tools to pry the latch.

trunk cable

tools

4 Dismantle the car's brake lights by yanking wires and pushing or kicking the lights out.

Then wave and yell to signal passersby or other cars. This method is also recommended if the car is moving and you need to signal cars behind you.

Be Aware

No car trunk is airtight, so the danger of suffocation in a car trunk is low. Breathe regularly and do not panic—panic increases the danger of your hyperventilating and passing out. Keep in mind, however, that on a hot day the interior temperature of a car trunk can reach 140 degrees. Work quickly but calmly.

HOW TO ESCAPE WHEN TIED UP

UPPER TORSO BONDS

1 When your captors start binding you, expand your body as much as possible.
- Take a deep breath, puff out your chest, and pull your shoulders back.
- Flex your arms against the bonds.
- Push against the bonds as much as possible.

2 When your captors are away, suck in your chest and stomach.

3 Wiggle free with the extra room you have given yourself.

HAND AND WRIST BONDS

1 Push or flex against the bonds as your captors are tying you.

2 Keep your wrists apart, if possible.

3 Use a pointed object that protrudes (a spike or hook) to work the bonds loose.
You may also be able to work the knots free with your teeth by biting and pulling on the knots.

Take a deep breath.

Flex against your bonds.

Keep your wrists apart.

Brace toes and knees together.

4 Free yourself by relaxing your hands and wrists and working until the slack can ride over your palms and fingertips.

Leg and Ankle Bonds

1 While being bound, flex your thighs, knees, calves, and ankles against the bonds.
- If being bound at the ankles, force them apart by bracing the toes of your shoes and knees together.
- If being bound at the thighs or calves, force them apart by keeping the toes of your feet together and your legs turned slightly outward.

2 Relax your legs and work the bonds down.
Use your hands to pull the bonds off your legs and ankles, even if your hands are bound.

Removing Gags

★ Rub your face or head against a wall, a piece of furniture, or anything projecting to slip the gag down over your chin.

HOW TO ESCAPE FROM A BAD DATE

FAKE AN EMERGENCY

1 Excuse yourself from the table.
Tell your date that you are going to the restroom to "wash up." Take your cell phone with you. If you do not have one, locate a restaurant phone that's out of your date's line of vision. Bring a restaurant matchbook or a business card that includes the restaurant's phone number.

2 Call a friend or relative for help.
Tell them to call you (either on your cell phone or on the restaurant's phone) and pretend there has been an emergency. Believable emergencies are:
- Personal Crisis: "My friend just broke up with her husband—she's having a breakdown. I have to go."
- Business Crisis: "My boss just called—she's in Seattle for a major presentation, and has lost all her files. I have to e-mail them to her immediately."
- Health Crisis: "My sister just called—our grandmother is alone and ill."

3 Leave quickly before your date can protest.
Apologize, but refuse any attempt your date makes to accompany you. If you leave swiftly and without hesitation, your date won't have time to understand what's happening or to object.

Slip Away Unnoticed

1 | Identify your escape route.
Observe your surroundings. Take note of the exits, especially the back doors. Look for the best way out and an alternative.

2 | Plan to alter your appearance.
Think about your most distinctive features and figure out how to hide or disguise them. The person you are trying to leave is going to see a figure moving past and away at a distance and will be focusing on the first impression. If you are not familiar to him and are uninteresting, you will not get a second look.

3 | Excuse yourself from the table.
Move to the restroom or any private area with a mirror to begin your transformation. Your date will probably wait only two or three minutes before expecting you to return, so act quickly, before he begins looking for you.

4 | Add or remove clothing.
Layering garments will change your body shape and even suggest a different gender. A long coat will obscure your body type. Hats are especially useful because they conceal your hair and facial features. Eyeglasses, whether added or removed, work wonders. A shopping bag is a handy prop and can be used to hold your belongings.

Add—or remove—eyeglasses. Roll or unroll your sleeves; tuck in or untuck your blouse. Modify your hairstyle.

5 | Change your walk and posture.
If you usually walk quickly, move slowly. If you stand up straight, hunch over. To alter your gait, slip a pebble in one shoe or bind one of your knees with a piece of string or cloth.

6 | Use or remove cosmetics.
Lipstick can change the shape of your mouth, heighten the color in your cheeks and nose, and even give you tired eyes if dabbed and blended on your eyelids. An eyebrow pencil can be used to add age lines, change the shape of your eyes and brows, or create facial hair.

7 | Change your hairstyle or color.
A rubberband, hairspray, water, or any gooey substance can be useful for changing a hairstyle, darkening your hair, or altering a hairline. Borrow flour from the kitchen to lighten or gray your hair color.

8 | Adopt a cover role.
A waiter in the restaurant may have an apron and be carrying a tray. If you can manage to procure these items, add or subtract a pair of eyeglasses and alter your hairline or hairstyle, you can become invisible as you are moving out of the restaurant, into the kitchen, and out the rear door. Or you can take on the role of a maintenance worker; carry a convenient potted plant out the front door and no one will think twice.

9 | Make your move.
Do not look at your date.

Slip Out the Window

If you do not think you will be able to change your appearance enough to slip past your date, you may have to find another way to depart. Back doors are the simplest; they are often located near the restrooms or are marked as fire exits. Do not open an emergency exit door if it is alarmed unless absolutely necessary; an alarm will only draw attention. If there are no accessible alternate doors, you will need to find a window.

1 **Locate a usable window.**
Avoid windows with chicken wire or large plate glass. Bathroom windows often work best. If you are not on the ground floor, be sure there is a fire escape.

2 **Attempt to open the window.**
Do not immediately break the window, no matter how dire your need to get out.

3 **Prepare to break the window if you cannot open it.**
Make sure no one is around. If you can, lock the bathroom door.

4 **Find an implement to break the window.**
Try to avoid using your elbow, fist, or foot. Suitable implements are:
• Wastebasket
• Toilet plunger
• Handbag or briefcase
• Paper towel dispenser

Strike the center of the glass with the implement.

5 Strike the center of the glass with the implement.
If the hand holding the implement will come within
a foot of the window as you break it, wrap it with a
jacket or sweater before attempting to break the glass.
If no implement is available, use your heavily wrapped
hand; be sure you wrap your arm as well, beyond the
elbow.

6 Punch out any remaining shards of glass.
Cover your fist with a jacket or sweater before removing the glass.

7 Make your escape.
Do not worry about any minor nicks and cuts. Run.

GET YOUR DATE TO LEAVE

1 Say something offensive.
If you know your date is of a particular religion or ethnicity, make inappropriate comments.

2 Behave inappropriately.
Do things that you think he will find unattractive or distasteful: chew with your mouth open, eat with your fingers, argue with the waiter, close your eyes and pretend to sleep, light matches and drop them on your plate, ignore everything he says, and/or call someone else on your cell phone.

3 Send your date on a "fool's errand."
• Tell him you want to go to a specific nightclub, but explain that it gets very crowded and that if you are not in line by a certain time (say, fifteen minutes from then), you won't get in. Tell your date that you have arranged to have your friend stop by the restaurant with guest passes, but that if your date does not go ahead to the nightclub to get in line, you'll never make it inside. If your date wants your cell phone number, give the number

willingly but make sure you change one digit. Promise you will see your date within half an hour. Never show.

- Fake an allergy attack, and insist that he leave in search of the appropriate over-the-counter allergy medicine. Explain that you must have been allergic to something in the drink/appetizer/food/taxicab, and that if you do not obtain your medicine you will break out in hives. When your date dutifully leaves, slip away.

Be Aware

Blind dates are the riskiest form of dating—it is best to check out a potential suitor extensively before the date.

- Have a friend agree to check out your potential suitor and call you before you enter the bar/restaurant. Send your friend in with a cell phone. Situate yourself at a bar nearby, and await her call. Have her contact you when she has identified the mark.
- If you discover unsavory facts about someone you're supposed to meet, call immediately to cancel the date. Blame work and say that you have to stay late at the office, or say that you're experiencing car trouble. A more permanent solution is to say that an old flame has reentered your life; this will prevent your blind date from calling you again and asking for a rain check.

How to Thwart an Affectionate Costumed Mascot

Keep a bench or child between yourself and the mascot. Shout "No!" and the mascot's name, if known. If unable to escape, crouch low to the ground, as the heavy plush fur of the mascot's suit may prevent him from bending down.

HOW TO FOIL
A UFO ABDUCTION

1 Do not panic.
The extraterrestrial biological entity (EBE) may sense your fear and act rashly.

2 Control your thoughts.
Do not think of anything violent or upsetting—the EBE may have the ability to read your mind. Try to avoid mental images of abduction (boarding the UFO, anal probes); such images may encourage them to take you.

3 Resist verbally.
Firmly tell the EBE to leave you alone.

4 Resist mentally.
Picture yourself enveloped in a protective shield of white light, or in a safe place. Telepathic EBEs may get the message.

5 Resist physically.
Physical resistance should be used only as a last resort. Go for the EBE's eyes (if they have any)—you will not know what its other, more sensitive areas are.

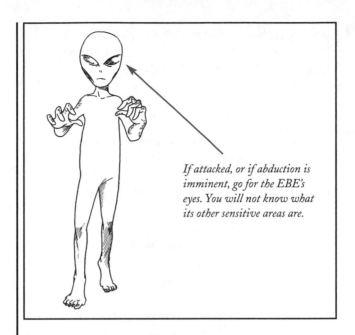

If attacked, or if abduction is imminent, go for the EBE's eyes. You will not know what its other sensitive areas are.

How to Report a UFO Sighting

1 Stay calm.
If you become upset or excited, you are likely to forget important details.

2 Accurately record the time at the start of the sighting, the time of any change of direction in the UFO's flight pattern, and the time at the end of the sighting.
If possible, use a mechanical stopwatch, since close proximity to a UFO may prevent electronic instruments from functioning correctly.

3 | Sketch a schematic of the UFO's path in the ground. Mark your position in the ground at the start of the sighting, and draw a line in the direction of the object when first seen, for each direction change, and when last seen.

4 | Try to identify any horizon landmarks with regard to the UFO's position.

5 | If you have a video or still camera, record the sighting.
Neither video nor still images carry much weight on their own, so it is essential that the images include reference information such as a tree, a mountain, or a skyline.

6 | Report the sighting as soon as possible.
Contact the UFO Reporting and Information Service, the Mutual UFO Network, or the National UFO Reporting Center.

Be Aware
Most sightings are in rural areas, away from bright lights, and near military installations. They occur most frequently during the summer months, around 9:00 P.M., with a secondary peak at around 3:00 A.M.

HOW TO SURVIVE IN A PLUMMETING ELEVATOR

1 Flatten your body against the car floor.

While there is disagreement among the experts, most recommend this method. This should distribute the force of impact, rather than concentrate it on one area of your body. (Standing may be difficult anyway.) Lie in the center of the car.

Lie flat on the floor in the center of the elevator, covering your head for protection.

2 | Cover your face and head to protect them from ceiling parts that may break loose.

Be Aware

- Hydraulic elevators are more likely than cable elevators to fall. These elevators are pushed from the bottom by a giant piston, similar to car jacks at service stations. Because the jack is subject to ground corrosion, it can rot, which could eventually cause the car to fall. The height of hydraulic elevators is limited to about 70 feet, so a free fall would probably result in injury—but not death.

- Elevators have numerous safety features. There have been very few recorded incidents involving death from plummeting elevators. In general, it is highly unlikely for a cable (also called traction) elevator to fall all the way to the bottom of the shaft. Moreover, the compressed air column in the elevator hoistway and the car buffers at the bottom of the hoistway may keep the forces of the impact survivable.

- Jumping just before the elevator hits the bottom is not a viable alternative. The chances that you will time your jump exactly right are infinitesimally small. Besides, the elevator will not remain completely intact when it hits—it will likely collapse around you and crush you if you are in the middle of your jump, or even if you are still standing.

HOW TO SNEAK OUT OF A MEETING

Sneak Out in Plain Sight

1 Establish your presence.
Lay the groundwork for your departure by first making a brief speech, giving a short presentation, or otherwise making your presence known. In this way people will remember that you were there.

2 Call attention to yourself.
Make a show of going out and then coming back into the meeting several times. Say, "Boy, this coffee really goes right through me!" and then go to the restroom twice. Make sure people notice when you return.

3 Make your escape.
The third time you leave, don't return.

Sneak Out Using a Distraction

1 Express interest in attending the meeting.
Before the meeting, say to your boss or a colleague, "I can't wait to see what Phil has to say" or, "Which conference room is the meeting in?" Make it clear that you really want this meeting and, thus, would be the last one to miss it.

2 | Sit away from the focus of attention.
Sit on the opposite end of the room from the person running the meeting or from the screen where the presentation will be displayed.

3 | Sneak out.
When the lights dim and the presentation begins, quietly get up from your seat. If there are empty chairs around the table, just walk away from your chair. If all the seats are taken, move your chair away from the table against a wall so the vacant chair will not be noticed. Leave the room and don't come back. Have a plausible cover story ready, such as an unexpected visit from a client/customer or a personal emergency regarding your spouse/child/pet.

CRAWL UNDER THE TABLE

1 | Assess the size and shape of the table.
The ideal conference table to escape is rectangular and seats at least 12 people, preferably more, with some of the seats left empty. People cluster at the center or at one end of the table if it is not full, usually leaving one or both ends available for an exit route. Do not attempt to sneak away under a round table since you may be surrounded by legs.

2 | Slide under the table.
When no one is looking, slide quietly down your chair to the floor. Push your chair against the wall or leave it in its place, depending on how full the table is (see step 3 above). Do not call attention to yourself.

Do not attempt to escape under a round table.

Crawl along the center of the table, avoiding your co-workers' feet.

3 | Crawl.
Proceed on your hands and knees under the center of the table. Avoid bumping shins, feet, or loose shoes. If you are discovered, say you are looking for your pen.

4 | Monitor conversation.
The end of the table will probably be closest to the door. Wait until someone at a long side of the table is speaking: People will look in that direction.

5 | Continue on all fours.
Crawl out from under the table and to the door. Reach up and open the door quietly. Check for people outside.

6 | Exit the room.
When the coast is clear, crawl into the hallway.

7 | Stand up and walk away.

Be Aware

- If you plan to escape by crawling, wear loose-fitting clothes.
- Most people have limited peripheral vision; when looking straight ahead, they cannot see an object at an angle of more than 45 degrees behind and to the side. Use this as a guide when determining if your escape will be noticed.
- If other escape plans will not work, spill a cup of lukewarm coffee on your pants. This strategy wins sympathy and also offers a perfect excuse for

leaving the meeting. If someone later asks why you never returned, say you got a slight burn. They probably will not seek to verify.

How to Stay Awake During a Meeting

★ **Use correct meeting posture.**
Keep your head up, shoulders back, and spine straight. Keep your legs bent at a 90-degree angle, not fully extended. Feet should be flat on the floor.

★ **Be on guard for mind-numbing repetition.**
Repetitive noise patterns and repetitive images can cause a trance-like state that deadens the senses. If phrases like "need better communication" and "building a team" are repeated, or if tables, graphs, and pie charts are projected endlessly, exit the room for a few minutes.

★ **Wear sunglasses.**
The harsh glare of fluorescent lights can cause eye strain and lead to fatigue. Wear dark glasses.

★ **Exercise.**
Exercise combats fatigue and keeps the mind alert. Take frequent walks around the room or do calisthenics. If possible, jog in place.

★ **Stay hydrated.**
Drink water or sports drinks that provide energy and contain potassium, salt, and carbohydrates. Coffee

contains caffeine, a stimulant that also acts as a diuretic, which will cause dehydration, so drink at least one glass of water for every cup of coffee you consume. This will also promote trips to the bathroom and, consequently, movement and stimulation. Do not drink alcohol: It depresses the nervous system and leads to fatigue.

 Use interrogation techniques.
Pinch yourself, sit in an uncomfortable position, poke your leg with a pen or paper clip, or stare wide-eyed at a bright light—the pain will heighten your awareness.

Be Aware
Warning signs of meeting fatigue include inattentiveness, back tension, shallow breathing, frequent blinking, heavy eyelids, and snoring.

HOW TO SURVIVE IF TRAPPED IN THE WORKPLACE

If kicking or banging on the door to the **bathroom, supply closet, walk-in-freezer,** or **lion cage** does not summon help immediately, save your energy for other means of egress.

IN A BATHROOM

BREAK THROUGH THE WALL

1 Tap on the wall until you hear a hollow sound.

Bang a hole in the wall large enough to crawl through.

2 Bang a hole in the wall.
Use a wooden plunger handle or other strong bathroom implement to poke at the wall. Avoid tiled areas. Continue jabbing and breaking the wall until you have opened a wide hole.

3 Crawl through.
Squeeze your body between the studs.

CLIMB OUT THROUGH THE CEILING

1 Push out the ceiling tiles.
Stand on the sink or other sturdy fixture. Push several drop-tile squares up and over to the side.

2 Look for pipes or other handholds.

3 Select a horizontal pipe that leads out of the bathroom.

4 Pull yourself up and onto the pipe.
Grab a pipe at least 6 inches in diameter. Pull up as you would for a chin-up, then swing your legs onto the pipe. Do not put your weight on the ceiling tiles or you risk falling through.

5 Crawl.
Shimmy along the pipe until you are no longer above the bathroom.

6 Kick out a ceiling tile and drop down into the hallway.

Pull yourself up on a pipe.

Be Aware

With ready access to water from the sink, you should be able to survive for days, if not weeks, in the bathroom, even without food.

1 Find a screwdriver.
If no screwdriver is available, look for a letter opener, bottle opener, tape dispenser, cocktail shaker, three-hole punch, or other metal implement with a flat end. A metal pen or strong plastic pen can also work.

2 Examine the door hinges.
Most doors open in and have the hinges on the inside. Locate the lower hinge.

3 Place the tip of the screwdriver under the top edge of the hinge pin.

Remove the hinge pins from the door.

4 Push or bang on the top of the handle of the screwdriver.
Pound with a hammer, shoe heel, table or chair leg, or other hard, unbreakable object.

5 Remove the pin from the hinge.

6 Remove the upper hinge.
Repeat steps 3 through 5.

7 Lift the door away from the door frame.
Pull on the hinge side first. You may be able to pull the door completely away from the frame.

8 Exit.

IN A WALK-IN FREEZER

1 Stay calm.
Panic wastes energy, which is warmth. The room's insulation and motor noise will likely prevent anyone from hearing your cries for help. Find a metal implement (keys or coins will work) and tap several times on the door to get someone's attention.

2 Check the door and lock area.
By law, all walk-in freezers and refrigerators must have an emergency release switch on the interior. Look on the door for a fluorescent knob that turns, or a lever that moves up and down.

3 | Locate a power switch.
Most units have a temperature control module on the inside, but it is likely to be well protected and may require tools to access. Some models may have an accessible on/off switch. If you can access the switch, turn off the cooling element.

4 | Locate boxes.
Tear cardboard boxes apart and spread the cardboard on the floor. The freezer's floor will be concrete or metal, and coming in contact with it will reduce your body temperature quickly.

5 | Look for insulating materials.
Many food items are packed in paper, plastic, foam peanuts, or straw. Lie down on the cardboard and cover yourself with insulating items to preserve body heat. Take care to cover your head completely: In cold conditions, an enormous amount of heat is lost through the head.

6 | Breathe slowly and stay put.
Take slow breaths and do not move around in the freezer or overexert yourself.

7 | Stay hydrated.
Suck on ice cubes or on frost from food parcels. Do not use body heat to melt frozen items or you risk hypothermia.

Use cardboard for insulation.

8 **Eat only if ice is available.**
Digestion requires water, so do not eat unless there is a sufficient supply of ice for you to melt. Eat ice cream or other foods intended to be eaten frozen. Avoid meats; these are likely to be frozen solid anyway.

9 **Tap on the door every 15 minutes until help arrives.**

Be Aware

- Do not attempt to disable the refrigeration mechanism. This may cause the unit to malfunction and leak noxious chemicals.
- Remain close to the ground. Although in most environments heat rises, the freezer will have a uniform temperature throughout, and the refrigeration mechanism is likely to be closer to the ceiling than at floor level.
- It is often customary to don a fur or other warm coat before entering a commercial freezer for any length of time. If you are wearing a coat, use it, but avoid over-exertion as you move around: Sweating causes the body to cool rapidly. If you feel yourself begin to sweat, open the coat slightly.
- Do not build a fire in an enclosed space.

IN A LION CAGE

IF THE LION IS NOT IMMEDIATELY VISIBLE

1 Quickly survey the cage.

Check to see if the lion is present. Most zoos have a large outdoor area for the lions to roam, and the lion may have wandered outside. The cage will be connected to this area through a small passage with a door that allows the cage to be sealed and cleaned while the lion is outside.

2 | Shut the door.
If a door is present and the lion is not, shut the door. If the lion is present, do not shut the door.

3 | Yell for help.

If the Lion Is Visible
1 | Do not run.
Even if the cage is large, or you feel you can safely make it to the passageway and through the door to the outdoor area, do not turn and run. This will only get the lion's attention, and there may be more lions outside.

2 | Stay still and calm.
Do not provoke the lion by moving around, running, or charging.

3 | Check for cubs.
A lioness guarding cubs will defend them fiercely, and may be more inclined to attack. If you see cubs, freeze.

4 | Check for food.
Lions are extremely protective of food, and even a lion with a full belly will protect his "kill." If the lion appears to be feeding or you notice fresh meat, do not approach the lion or its food.

5 | Observe the lion's eyes and tail.
A lion in a zoo will be desensitized to the presence of humans and may not attack immediately. Lions have different temperaments, however, and can range from

passive to highly aggressive. Even a passive lion is likely to eventually attack a stranger in its cage. If the lion meets your gaze and its tail begins to twitch, the lion is getting ready to attack.

6 | Listen for a growl.
A low staccato growl, combined with eye contact and a lashing tail, usually indicates that an attack is likely.

7 | Find a defensive tool.
Moving very slowly, pick up anything within reach: a water bowl, bench, or anything else that may be used to fend off a charge.

8 | Back away slowly.
Moving carefully, back toward the door of the cage. Using a quiet but firm voice, tell someone to open the cage or, if impossible, to get the lion keeper immediately.

9 | Watch for mock charges.
A lion may make several "mock" charges before actually attacking. It will run forward suddenly, then stop. It may back away before charging again. Mock-charging is an indication that a real attack is imminent. Stand your ground and be ready.

10 | Yell.
Yell as loud as you can. Lions are sensitive to loud noises and yelling may discourage one from further charges.

Watch for signs of imminent attack: twitching tail, eye contact, and growling.

11 | Fend off attack.
If the lion attacks, use a bench, bowl, or any other object to push its paws and head away from you.

12 | Yell for help.
Keep screaming as loudly as possible.

HOW TO SURVIVE
IF YOU ARE
BURIED ALIVE

1 Conserve your air supply.

If you are buried in a typical coffin, you will have enough air to survive for an hour or two at most. Take deep breaths, then hold for as long as possible before exhaling. Do not breathe and then swallow, which will lead to hyperventilation. Do not light a match or lighter. Combustion will quickly use your available oxygen. It is safe to use a flashlight if you have one. Do not yell. Yelling will lead to panic, which will increase your heart rate and lead to fast breathing that will rapidly consume your air supply.

2 Press up on the coffin lid with your hands.

An inexpensive "pine box" (chipboard coffin) or a recycled paperboard coffin will have some give to it, so it will be relatively easy to break through. If you feel flex in the coffin lid, continue to step 3. A metal-clad or hardwood coffin will be impossible to pierce. In this case, your only hope is to signal for rescue. Use a metal object (ring, belt buckle, coin, flask, pen) to signal that you are alive. Tap SOS, the international distress signal, on the coffin lid: three quick taps, followed by three slower taps, followed by three quick taps. Continue to repeat the distress call until someone hears you.

3 Remove your shirt.
Cross your arms over your chest, then uncross your arms so that your elbows are bent and your hands are at your shoulders. Pull your shirt up and off your head from the shoulders, do a partial sit-up (as much as you can in the space available), then pull your shirt over your head and off.

4 Tie the bottom of the shirt in a knot.
The shirt should have only one large opening, at the neck, as does a bag.

5 Place your head through the neck hole.
The knot should be on the top of your head. The shirt will prevent you from suffocating on loose earth.

6 Break through the coffin.
Using your feet, begin kicking the coffin lid. A cheap coffin may have already split from the weight of the earth above, making your job easier. Break apart the lid with your hands and feet and let the loose dirt rush in.

7 Use your hands to push the dirt toward your feet.
There should be some space at the bottom end of the coffin, below your feet. As the dirt rushes in, work quickly but calmly to fill the space at your feet. When this space fills up, push dirt to your sides. Breathe slowly and regularly.

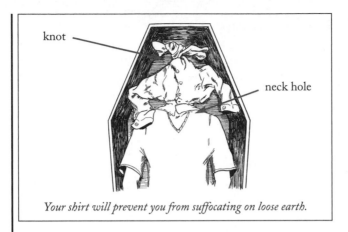

knot

neck hole

Your shirt will prevent you from suffocating on loose earth.

8 Sit up.

As you move to a seated position, the loose earth above will move to fill the space you just occupied. As the dirt falls, continue to push it into the coffin until you can stand up.

9 Stand.

Once you are standing, you should be able to push the dirt above you up and out of the grave. When you have cleared all the dirt above you, climb out.

Be Aware

- A recently interred coffin will be covered with loose earth that is relatively easy to dig through.
- Escaping from a coffin interred during a rain storm will be difficult. The compacted weight of the wet earth will make digging almost impossible.
- The higher the clay content of the soil, the more difficult your escape will be.

HOW TO ESCAPE FROM QUICKSAND

1 When walking in quicksand country, carry a stout pole—it will help you get out should you need to.

2 As soon as you start to sink, lay the pole on the surface of the quicksand.

3 Flop onto your back on top of the pole. After a minute or two, equilibrium in the quicksand will be achieved, and you will no longer sink.

4 Work the pole to a new position: under your hips and at right angles to your spine. The pole will keep your hips from sinking, as you (slowly) pull out first one leg and then the other.

5 Take the shortest route to firmer ground, moving slowly.

How to Avoid Sinking

Quicksand is just ordinary sand mixed with upwelling water, which makes it behave like a liquid. However, quicksand—unlike water—does not easily let go. If you try to pull a limb out of quicksand, you have to work against the vacuum left behind. Following are a few tips:

- The viscosity of quicksand increases with shearing—move slowly so the viscosity is as low as possible.
- Floating on quicksand is relatively easy and is the best way to avoid its clutches. You are more buoyant in quicksand than you are in water. Humans are less dense than freshwater, and saltwater is slightly more dense. Floating is easier in saltwater than freshwater and much easier in quicksand. Spread your arms and legs far apart and try to float on your back.

When in an area with quicksand, bring a stout pole and use it to put your back into a floating position.

Place the pole at a right angle from your spine to keep your hips afloat.

HOW TO
SURVIVE A RIOT

1 Remain indoors if you learn about any nearby rioting or civil unrest.

Avoid the windows. Listen for reports on radio or television. If you hear gunfire, try to find out where the shooting is located. Use the telephone if it is still functioning, or ask an official or your hotel manager for information.

2 If you believe the crisis is unresolvable or seriously threatens your life, plan to leave the country quickly.

3 Determine the best route to the airport or embassy, and leave the building through any safe exit.

Make sure that the airport is operating before you travel there. If you cannot make it to your own country's embassy, plan to head for the embassy of an allied nation.

4 Wear clothing in muted tones.

Put on a long-sleeve shirt, jacket, jeans, a hat, socks, and lightweight boots. (Although you may be in a tropical or warm part of the world, it gets quite cold on planes, and you may have to sleep in an airport or connect to a flight landing in a colder region.)

5 Exit away from gunfire or mobs.

Select a way out that is not easily observed. Exits include windows, vents, or even the roof.

6 Leave as a group.

Especially if you have to dash across an open area, such as the front of a building, a wide street, or a plaza, you are safer with company. Snipers or enemies will have multiple objects to focus on, not just one, and will not be as likely to make a move.

7 Do not run.

Unless your life is in imminent danger, walk. Walking is harder for the eye to detect: The human eye can quickly sight someone running. Running can also generate excitement—people may chase you.

8 If you must travel by car, be prepared for evasive maneuvers.

Drive on back streets, not main roads, and be prepared to abandon the car if the situation becomes critical. Watch out for checkpoints, roundabouts, major intersections, and military/police barracks. Do not stop for anything—remember the car can be a useful 2,000-pound weapon that even a mob cannot stop. If you cannot drive forward, drive in reverse.

A reliable driver who knows the area will be able to navigate much better than you. If no driver or taxi is available, hire a local to drive your car for you. (You may need to promise to give your car in exchange.) Abandon the car outside the embassy or airport.

If a Molotov cocktail (flammable liquid in a glass container with a lighted wick) hits your car, speed up—it may burn out as you gain speed.

Drive on back streets, not main roads, and be prepared to abandon your car if necessary. Get to an airport or friendly embassy.

9 If you encounter unavoidable roadblocks, be prepared to bargain your way to safety.

You might need to give up everything you are carrying in order to get away. Offer cash first, equipment (watches, cameras, jewelry) second.

10 Get to an embassy or to the airport as soon as possible.

Be Aware

- If you are in a volatile region where there is a likelihood of civil disorder, be prepared for a rapid evacuation. Each person and family member should have an escape pack set aside near the front door. A good, small backpack is preferable to any type of luggage. It should contain the following:

FLASHLIGHT. Pack a mini-flashlight with extra batteries. Affix a red or blue lens if you have one; red or blue light is difficult for observers (snipers, mobs) to see at night.

SMALL COMPASS AND A DETAILED MAP OF THE CITY. Be sure to mark the embassy and helicopter landing zones on the map.

KNIFE. Include a small pocketknife for cutting.

FIRE-STARTING TOOL. Carry storm-safe matches or a lighter in a waterproof bag. Pack small baggies of dryer lint, which is light and highly flammable.

BLACK GARBAGE BAGS. Use these for emergency shelter and camouflage.

WATER AND FOOD. Carry at least two quarts of water per person. Bring only high-energy or instant foods. Do not eat unless you have water.

• Conceal on your person, in a multi-pocket neck pouch, the following items:

MONEY. Take $25 in single U.S. dollars and all of your local currency and divide it among your pouch and pockets. This will serve as bribe money for checkpoints. Dole it out in heaps until it appears you have no more. Do not offer your papers. Carry more money in your neck pouch, but keep the bulk of your cash in your socks, crotch, or ankle pouch.

Passport. Place a full photocopy of your passport in the main section of the pouch for easy access. Keep your original passport in a separate section. Show the copy to locals who demand it. Never give up the original.

Official documents. Visas, phone numbers, proof of citizenship, birth certificates, and so on should be kept with your original passport.

Soft earplugs. Helicopters are very noisy, and earplugs are useful when you want to sleep in a battle zone.

CHAPTER 3

ILLNESS AND INJURY

HOW TO FALL DOWN A FLIGHT OF STAIRS

1 | Lower your center of gravity.
When you sense yourself falling, crouch low to the floor.

2 | Do not attempt to break your fall.
Avoid using your hands to try to break your initial fall. The weight of your body, in conjunction with the gravitational forces of the fall, may break your wrists.

3 | Move to the inside wall.
As you fall, keep your body close to the wall of the stairway, if there is one. You are more likely to catch an arm or a leg in the banister (or fall through or over it) than to injure yourself on the wall.

4 | Tuck.
Move your arms, legs, hands, and knees in close to your body. Tuck your chin to your chest. With your elbows tucked in, place your hands on the sides of your head.

5 | Roll in a zigzag pattern.
Concentrate on rolling on your major muscle groups: lats (back), deltoids (shoulders), quads (thighs), and gluteus maximus (rear end). Avoid rolling head

Roll in toward the wall on one shoulder,
then out toward the banister on the other.

over heels, straight down: Your increasing momentum
may cause injury, even with your body positioned correctly. Instead, roll in toward the wall on one shoulder, then out toward the banister on the other. Repeat
the pattern until you reach the bottom. A zigzag roll
will help you reduce speed and maintain control. Do
not attempt the zigzag roll on a stairway with an old,
rickety banister, an open railing, or no banister at all.

6 Check for injury.
Do not get up immediately. Slowly move each limb in
turn to make sure nothing is broken. If you are in
extreme pain, yell for help.

How to Survive
Falling Through a Floor

Spread your arms wide to distribute your weight across unbroken flooring. Place your palms down and push your body up and back, away from the hole. If you are in the hole up to your waist or farther, lean forward onto your forearms and push to raise as much of your body mass as possible above the hole. Repeat until free. Do not grasp at furniture legs above the hole or kick with your legs below.

HOW TO
TAKE A PUNCH

A Blow to the Body

1   Tighten your stomach muscles.
A body blow to the gut (solar plexus) can damage organs and kill. This sort of punch is one of the best and easiest ways to knock someone out. (Harry Houdini died from an unexpected blow to the abdomen.)

2   Do not suck in your stomach if you expect that a punch is imminent.

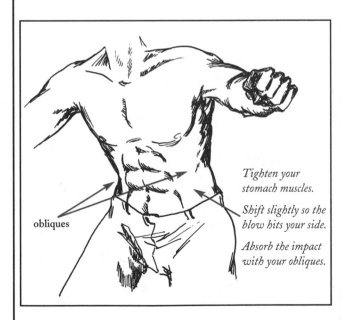

obliques

Tighten your stomach muscles.

Shift slightly so the blow hits your side.

Absorb the impact with your obliques.

3 | If possible, shift slightly so that the blow hits your side, but do not flinch or move away from the punch.

Try to absorb the blow with your obliques: this is the set of muscles on your side that wraps around your ribs. While a blow to this area may crack a rib, it is less likely to do damage to internal organs.

A Blow to the Head

1 | Move toward the blow, not away from it.

Getting punched while moving backward will result in the head taking the punch at full force. A punch to the face can cause head whipping, where the brain moves suddenly inside the skull, and may result in severe injury or death.

2 | Tighten your neck muscles and clench your jaw to avoid scraping of the upper and lower palates.

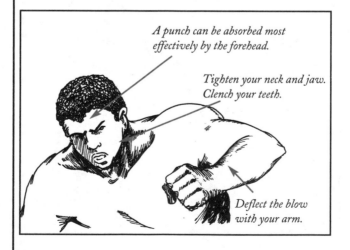

A punch can be absorbed most effectively by the forehead.

Tighten your neck and jaw. Clench your teeth.

Deflect the blow with your arm.

A Straight Punch

1 The straight punch—one that comes straight at your face—should be countered by moving toward the blow.
This will take force from the blow.

2 A punch can be absorbed most effectively and with the least injury by the forehead.
Avoid taking the punch in the nose, which is extremely painful.

3 Attempt to deflect the blow with an arm.
Moving into the punch may result in your attacker missing the mark wide to either side.

4 (optional) Hit back with an uppercut or roundhouse.

A Roundhouse Punch

1 Clench your jaw.
A punch to the ear causes great pain and can break your jaw.

2 Move in close to your attacker.
Try to make the punch land harmlessly behind your head.

3 (optional) Hit back with an uppercut.

An Uppercut

1 Clench your neck and jaw.
An uppercut can cause much damage, whipping your head back, easily breaking your jaw or your nose.

2 Use your arm to absorb some of the impact or deflect the blow to the side—anything to minimize the impact of a straight punch to the jaw.

3 Do not step into this punch.
If possible, move your head to the side.

4 (optional) Hit back with a straight punch to the face or with an uppercut of your own.

HOW TO TAKE A BULLET

1 | Face the shooter.
You do not want to take the bullet in your back or the base of your skull.

2 | Get low.
In addition to making yourself a smaller target, by keeping a low profile you will be better able to protect your head, neck, and midline—all areas where a bullet wound is most likely to cause fatal injury or permanent disability.

3 | Sit.
Sit with your rear end on the ground. Bend your knees and keep your legs in front of you, protecting your midline with your shins and thighs.

4 | Move your elbows into the center of your body.
Place both forearms in front of you, covering your face.

5 | Place your hands over your head.
Hold your fingers together, with your palms toward you. Keep your hands an inch or two in front of you to absorb the impact of the bullet.

6 | Wait for the impact.
You may notice little more than a "punch" sensation, or you may feel nothing at all.

7 | Determine the site of the injury.
Bullet wounds in the hands and feet, lower legs, and forearms are rarely fatal, provided blood loss is controlled.

8 | Control the bleeding.
Place firm, direct pressure on the wound to slow blood loss. If the bullet entered an appendage and pressure does not stop the bleeding, use a belt or narrow strip of cloth as a tourniquet. Place the tourniquet on the affected limb, several inches above the injury site. It should be tight enough to stop heavy blood flow. A tourniquet may cause permanent damage to the affected limb, and should be used only as a last resort. Never leave a tourniquet in place for more than a few minutes.

9 | Get help.
Seek medical attention as soon as possible.

Be Aware

- If you are crouching next to a wall, stay a foot or more away from the surface. Bullets will skid along the wall after impact.
- Gunshot wounds to the neck are almost always fatal.
- Most interior walls and doors (including car doors) will not stop a bullet larger than .22 or .25 caliber.

HOW TO SURVIVE A
ROLLOVER IN A CAR

1 Use your legs to brace your lower body.
You will have just fractions of a second to prepare for
impact. Remove your feet from the pedals, placing the
soles of your feet flat against the sheet metal behind
the pedals. Using your leg muscles, press hard against
the metal surface, as if you are on a leg press. Extend
your legs as far as possible, pressing your body back
into the seat.

2 Push your upper body against the seat.
Using both hands, grab the wheel at the three and
nine o'clock positions and grip tightly. Push out with
your arms, pressing your torso as far into the seat back
as possible. Keep your elbows tucked in to your body.

3 Secure your head and neck.
Press the back of your head and neck into the head-
rest as far as they will go.

4 Tense all of your muscles.
Exert as much force as possible to move your entire
body back into the seat, which is your best protection
during the rollover.

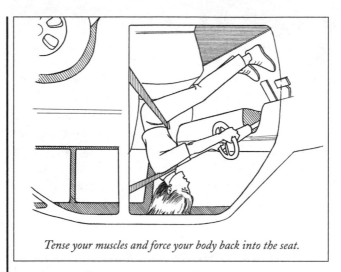
Tense your muscles and force your body back into the seat.

5 If the car lands upright and the engine is still running, steer the car away from obstructions or oncoming traffic.
Because they have a lower center of gravity than trucks and SUVs, cars tend to roll over completely and land on their wheels.

6 If the car lands on its roof, turn off the ignition.
Most modern cars (those manufactured after 1985) have a cutoff switch that kicks in automatically to stop fuel flow to the engine when the vehicle senses a rollover. If the engine is still running, turn it off.

7 Carefully remove your seat belt.
You will be hanging upside down, with your safety belt holding you in your seat. Brace your hands and feet against the roof before unlatching the belt.

In a single-vehicle rollover with no collision, your primary (steering wheel) air bag may not have deployed. Any side curtain air bags and head protection systems will have deployed, however, so watch for hot gas escaping from these devices.

8 Escape from the car.
The vehicle's steel safety cage and roll bars may have preserved the integrity of the car, keeping the doors in working condition. If you cannot open the door, crawl through the window. If the window has not been broken during the rollover and is intact, try to roll it down. If you are unable to do so, use a metal object such as a steering wheel lock to break the glass.

9 Run.
Move away from the car as quickly as possible in case there is a fuel leak, which could cause an explosion.

Be Aware

- SUVs and trucks have less-stringent safety standards than cars and tend to have a higher center of gravity, making them more prone to a rollover.
- The roofs of early-model SUVs and trucks may be deformed in a rollover.
- When occupants are wearing seat belts during a rollover, most injuries are to the head (from hitting the roof supports) and arms (from being flung out the windows by rollover forces). When occupants are not wearing seat belts, they will most likely be thrown from the vehicle.

HOW TO SURVIVE
AN AIRPLANE CRASH

To Decrease the Odds of a Crash

1 Take a nonstop flight, if possible.
Most accidents happen in the takeoff and landing
phases of flight; the fewer stops you make, the less
chance of an accident.

2 Watch the skies.
Many accidents involve severe weather. As takeoff
time approaches, check the weather along the route,
particularly in places where you will land. Consider
delaying your flight if the weather could be severe.

3 Wear long-sleeved shirts and long pants made of
natural fibers.
Radiant heat and flash burns can be avoided if you put
a barrier between you and the heat. Avoid easy-care
polyester or nylon: most synthetic materials that aren't
specifically treated to be fire resistant will melt at relatively low temperatures (300 to 400 degrees Fahren-
heit). Synthetic fabrics will usually shrink before they
melt, and if they are in contact with skin when this
happens, they will make the burn—and its treatment—much more serious. Wear closed-toe, hard-
soled shoes; you might have to walk through twisted,
torn metal or flames. In many cases, people survive the
crash, but are killed or injured by post-impact fire and
its by-products, like smoke and toxic gases.

4 Select a seat on the aisle, somewhere in the rear half of the cabin.

The odds of surviving a crash are higher in the middle-to-rear section compared to the middle-to-front section of the cabin. An aisle seat offers the easiest escape route access, unless you are sitting right next to an emergency exit: If you can get a window seat right next to the emergency exit, this is a better choice.

5 Listen to the safety briefing and locate your nearest exits.

Most airplane accident survivors had listened to the briefing and knew how to get out of the plane. Pick an exit to use in an emergency, and an alternate in case the first one is not available.

6 Count the seats between you and the exits in case smoke fills the plane and you cannot see them.

Make sure you understand how the exit doors work and how to operate them.

7 Practice opening your seat belt a few times.

Many people mistakenly try to push the center of the buckle rather than pull up on it.

TO PREPARE FOR A CRASH

1 Make sure that your seat belt is tightly fastened and that your chair back is fully upright.

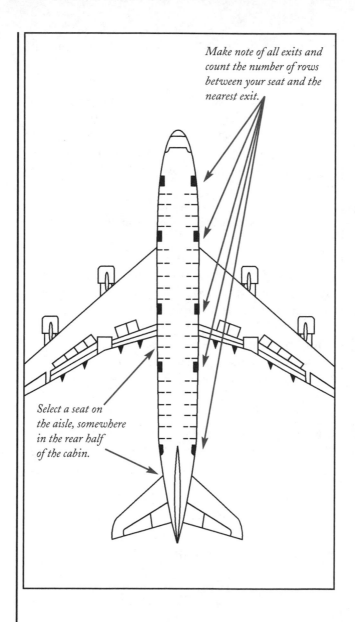

Make note of all exits and count the number of rows between your seat and the nearest exit.

Select a seat on the aisle, somewhere in the rear half of the cabin.

2 | Bend forward with one arm across your knees.

3 | Place your pillow in your lap and hold your head against the pillow with your free arm.

4 | Push your legs forward and brace for impact by placing your feet or knees against the chair in front of you.
If you are over water, loosen your shirt (and tie) so that your movement is not restricted when you attempt to swim. Be ready for two jolts: when the plane first hits water and when the nose hits water again.

5 | Stay calm and be ready to help yourself.
The vast majority of crash survivors were able to get out either under their own power or with the help of someone already on the plane. Fire and rescue personnel are unlikely to enter the airplane to pull you out.

6 | Do not take anything with you.
If you have something you absolutely cannot part with, you should keep it in your pocket and not in your carry-on baggage.

7 | Stay low if the plane is on fire.
Follow the exit procedures described in the safety briefing. Illuminated floor lights should indicate the exits: the lights are red where exit rows exist.

how to survive an airplane crash

HOW TO PERFORM A TRACHEOTOMY

This procedure, technically called a cricothyroid-otomy, should be undertaken only when a person with a throat obstruction is not able to breathe at all—no gasping sounds, no coughing—and only after you have attempted to perform the Heimlich maneuver three times without dislodging the obstruction. If possible, someone should call for paramedics while you proceed.

WHAT YOU WILL NEED

- A first aid kit, if available
- A razor blade or very sharp knife
- A straw (two would be better) or a ballpoint pen with the inside (ink-filled tube) removed. If neither a straw nor a pen is available, use stiff paper or cardboard rolled into a tube. Good first aid kits may contain "trache" tubes.

There will not be time for sterilization of your tools, so do not bother; infection is the least of your worries at this point.

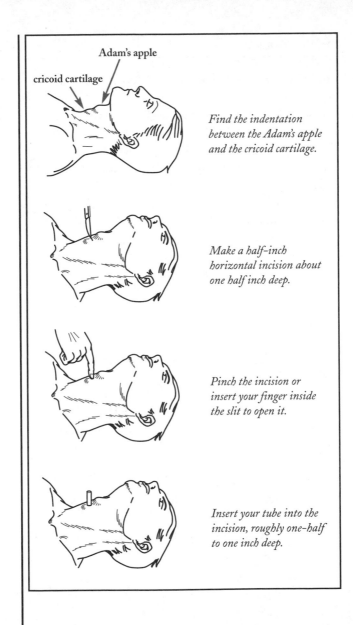

Adam's apple

cricoid cartilage

Find the indentation between the Adam's apple and the cricoid cartilage.

Make a half-inch horizontal incision about one half inch deep.

Pinch the incision or insert your finger inside the slit to open it.

Insert your tube into the incision, roughly one-half to one inch deep.

how to perform a tracheotomy

How to Proceed

1 Find the person's Adam's apple (thyroid cartilage).

2 Move your finger about one inch down the neck until you feel another bulge.
This is the cricoid cartilage. The indentation between the two is the cricothyroid membrane, where the incision will be made.

3 Take the razor blade or knife and make a half-inch horizontal incision.
The cut should be about half an inch deep. There should not be too much blood.

4 Pinch the incision open or place your finger inside the slit to open it.

5 Insert your tube in the incision, roughly one-half to one inch deep.

6 Breathe into the tube with two quick breaths.
Pause five seconds, then give one breath every five seconds.

7 You will see the chest rise and the person should regain consciousness if you have performed the procedure correctly.
The person should be able to breathe on their own, albeit with some difficulty, until help arrives.

HOW TO SURVIVE
A FLU PANDEMIC

⭐ **Wear a surgical mask in public.**
Influenza is a virus that enters the body through contact with mucous membranes, so you must protect your nose and mouth. If you cannot get a mask, keep a bandanna tied securely over your nose and mouth. Do not touch or rub your eyes, nose, or mouth.

⭐ **Restrict and ration towel usage.**
Each member of the household should have an assigned towel, washcloth, dishcloth, and pillow. (All household members should sleep in separate bedrooms, if possible.) Label towels with masking tape to avoid mix-ups. Wash all towels with bleach.

⭐ **Sneeze and cough into your elbow.**
Sneezing and coughing into your elbow will prevent germs from reaching your hands and being spread through contact. Recommend that others follow suit.

⭐ **Keep your hands clean.**
When washing hands in a public restroom, first pull the lever on the towel dispenser to lower a towel, then wash your hands. Rip off the dispensed towel, then use it to pull the dispenser lever again and to turn off the water faucet. Discard the first towel. Tear off the second towel and use it to dry your hands and open the bathroom door, then discard.

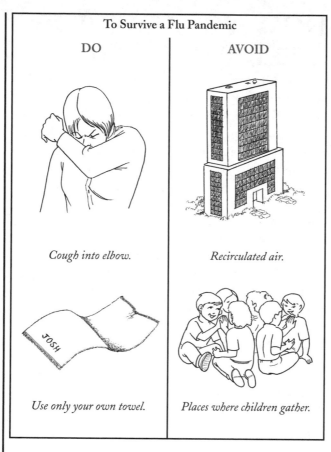

To Survive a Flu Pandemic

DO	AVOID
Cough into elbow.	*Recirculated air.*
Use only your own towel.	*Places where children gather.*

 Sanitize before touching areas with high germ potential.

Disinfect light switches, doorknobs, keyboards and mice, telephone receivers, refrigerator door handles, sink faucets, and the flush handle on the toilet. Do not use public telephones.

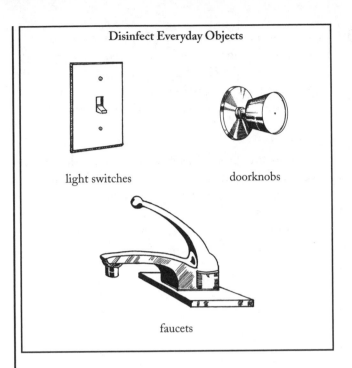

Disinfect Everyday Objects

light switches

doorknobs

faucets

⭐ **Empty the trash often.**
Do not let used tissues pile up in wastebaskets; they may carry the flu. Wear rubber gloves when emptying trash. Wash the gloves frequently, or throw them out after each use and get a new pair.

⭐ **Avoid areas with recirculated air systems.**
Do not get on an airplane. Avoid entering buildings that use recirculation systems designed to reduce fuel consumption. (In the United States, many such structures were erected during the 1970s energy crisis.)

⭐ **Do not enter areas where people congregate.**
Hospitals, prisons, day-care centers, college dorms, movie theaters, checkout lines, and other places where large numbers of people cohabitate or group closely together should be avoided during the pandemic.

Be Aware
- Get a flu shot as soon as they become available.
- Wash hands frequently and immediately upon returning home from being outdoors.
- Not all masks are equally effective. For best protection, use an N95 "respirator" mask that completely covers the nose, mouth, and chin.

chapter 3: illness and injury

HOW TO TREAT
FOOD POISONING

1 Stay hydrated.
The symptoms of food poisoning vary depending on the type of microorganism or toxin ingested, but can generally cause severe stomach cramping, fever, vomiting, and diarrhea, leading to dehydration. Drink several gallons of water per day.

2 Replenish mineral salts.
Eat bland foods, in moderation, as soon as you are able. Diarrhea depletes the body of salts, and drinking water alone will not replace them; sports rehydration drinks are effective. Nibble on dry salted crackers or plain rice to replenish salts, too.

3 Do not induce vomiting.
Depending on the microorganism or toxin involved, food poisoning may cause vomiting, which does not clear the bacteria from the body, but will cause further dehydration.

4 Do not take anti-peristaltic medication.
Some anti-diarrhea medications work by slowing the movement of waste in the gut, causing the toxins to remain in the body for a longer period of time.

5 | Avoid alcohol, spicy foods, and milk products.
These drinks and foods may aggravate the gut and cause additional gas and cramping. Never follow a suspect meal with a drink of alcohol to "kill" the germs; this is not effective.

6 | Be prepared for several days of discomfort.
Food poisoning may induce a severe headache and sweating. Keep the body cool: Never try to sweat out the germs. The symptoms of food poisoning are usually short-lived. If the symptoms persist for more than a week, or if you detect bleeding, consult a health care professional.

HOLIDAY FOOD ALERT

★ | Oysters should be fully cooked.
Raw oysters are particularly susceptible to invasions by microorganisms that can cause food poisoning: If the raw oyster tastes "off" in any way, do not swallow it.

★ | Fully cook all meat.
Poultry should be fully cooked, with no traces of pink or red, to an internal temperature of 165°F. Beef and game should be cooked to at least 140°F.

★ | Serve cooked foods immediately.
Cooked foods that are not served immediately must be kept at a holding temperature between 140° and 165°F. Do not leave food unrefrigerated longer than two hours or the chances of bacterial growth increase.

Foods That Pose a Special Risk of Food Poisoning

oysters   ham

turkey   shrimp cocktail

eggnog   damaged canned foods

⭐ **Egg yolks should not be eaten raw or runny.**
This will reduce the risk of salmonella poisoning. Eggnog usually contains raw egg yolks, so make sure the eggnog you drink has been pasteurized. Homemade mayonnaise is made with raw eggs, so avoid it.

⭐ **Cooked shellfish should be kept on ice.**
Fish and seafood, especially shellfish, are often harbor to many different kinds of microorganisms.

⭐ **Avoid any dented cans.**
If the seal on the can has been affected, the contents may be contaminated and you risk getting botulism.

Be Aware

- Food poisoning is caused by a range of micro-organisms or their byproducts. Each bug has its own properties and set of symptoms: Some must be alive and present in large quantities to cause harm, while others, such as *E. coli* 0157, can inflict a lethal dose from just a few bacteria.
- Separate raw and cooked foods. Even foods that have been properly cooked can be contaminated if they come in contact with raw foods or implements (knives and cutting boards, for example) that have touched them.
- Drink bottled water when traveling to visit relatives if you are unsure of the safety of the tap water. Avoid ice cubes, as these are usually made with tap water. Check seals on bottles to make sure they are intact: If they are broken, the bottles may have been refilled with tap water.

HOW TO IDENTIFY UNSAFE CAFETERIA FOOD

Meat and Poultry

★ Check the color.
When fully cooked, beef turns brown or gray; chicken is white or brown without a trace of pink or red (depending on whether it is light or dark meat); and pork is also white, with no tinge of pink or red. If you cannot identify what kind of meat you are being served, do not eat it. No meat or poultry should ever be yellow, blue, or green.

★ Check the temperature.
Hot foods should be piping hot; cold foods should be chilled. If the temperature is in doubt, ask a food service operator for a cooking thermometer and stick it into the center of the item. Hot meats should be at least 145°F, cold foods no warmer than 40°F.

★ Poke with a fork.
If the juices run red, the meat is undercooked.

★ Look at the gravy.
Sauces and gravies may have a thick "skin" or float in a puddle of congealed oil. These items are a breeding ground for bacteria.

how to identify unsafe cafeteria food

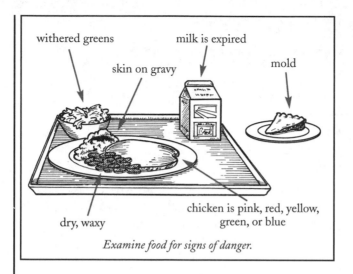

withered greens

milk is expired

mold

skin on gravy

chicken is pink, red, yellow, green, or blue

dry, waxy

Examine food for signs of danger.

SALAD BAR

⭐ Look for a sneeze guard.
Salad bars and other self-serve areas should have plastic guards to protect food from germs. Avoid foods in areas without these protective devices.

⭐ Watch for slow food turnover.
Food left out too long will have a dry, waxy, or withered appearance. Food should not be left out from breakfast to lunch and lunch to dinner. If you suspect slow turnover, mark a piece of food with a carefully placed garnish; parsley works well. Return to the dining hall later in the day to see if your marked item is still present. If it is, complain to management or the chef.

⭐ **Avoid foods that need to be eaten soon after being cooked.**
Scrambled eggs should not sit in a steam tray for more than two hours; hardboiled eggs keep at room temperature for two hours or for up to one week if refrigerated.

Packaged Foods

⭐ **Check the expiration date.**
If it is past the date shown on the package, do not eat it. This applies to yogurt, milk, sushi, and any prepared or packaged foods.

⭐ **Check the package for damage.**
If the seal is broken or the package looks damaged, do not eat the contents. Gently squeeze the bag of chips or pretzels to see if the bag holds air and remains firm. For vacuum-sealed jars, make sure the top has not popped up, which would indicate that the jar has been opened and the contents may be unsafe to eat. Do not eat food from dented cans—the sharp point of the dent may allow air and germs into the can.

Be Aware
- Watch for overripe fruits and vegetables.
  Extensive brown or black spots are not good.
- Check bread and pies for mold. Green means STOP.

HOW TO CURE INSOMNIA

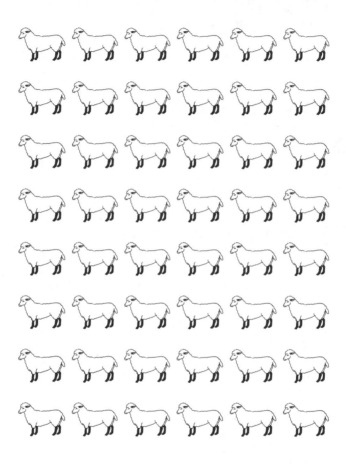

Take a warm bath; eat a bedtime snack; drink warm milk or herbal tea; cover illuminated clocks; lie on your back; rub your stomach; flex your toes. To prevent insomnia, avoid caffeine, nicotine, and alcohol. Light exercise or stretching an hour before bed can help relax muscle tension. Count sheep.

HOW TO DEAL
WITH "THE SPINS"

1 Focus your gaze on a stationary object in the room.
Keep your eyes open. Avoid looking at ceiling fans.
Stare at the object for one minute.

2 Close your eyes.

3 Picture the object you were looking at.
Imagine that the object is imprinted on the inside of
your eyelids.

4 Open your eyes.
If the spinning returns, stare at your object for one
minute.

5 Close your eyes.
Repeat steps 3 and 4.

6 Repeat steps 3, 4, and 5 until the spinning stops or
you pass out.

Be Aware
• The spins usually occur when your eyes are closed.
Watch television, go out for some air, or eat a
meal—anything to stay awake and keep your eyes
open until you sober up.

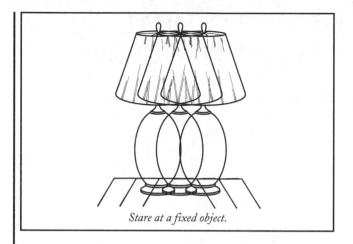

Stare at a fixed object.

- Eating reduces drinking-related sickness by reducing the speed at which alcohol in the stomach is absorbed into the bloodstream. Eat before drinking: Once you have the spins, it is too late.
- Alcohol is a diuretic and dehydrates. After drinking, replace lost fluid, vitamins, and electrolytes by consuming sports drinks. Avoid drinking excessive amounts of plain water, which will dilute the sodium concentration in the body.

How to Vomit Correctly

1 Be prepared.
Vomiting may be preceded by sweating, nausea, gagging, increased saliva, or the sensation of swelling under the tongue.

2 | **Move quickly.**
Get to a quiet bathroom or a private area with an appropriate receptacle, such as a toilet, trash can, or metal bowl. If outdoors, look for an area secluded by trees or bushes. Avoid public spaces.

3 | **Remove necktie or necklace.**

4 | **Open collar.**
Unbutton your shirt at least two buttons and pull the sides apart. If you are wearing a pullover, remove it completely, if time permits. Tie back long hair.

5 | **Relax.**
Do not resist.

6 | **Target a destination.**
Vomit into the receptacle. If vomiting into a toilet, grip the sides for support.

7 | **Wait.**
The first bout of vomiting may not be the last. Wait several minutes to make sure you remain in control.

8 | **Clean up.**
Wash your hands and face, rinse out your mouth, and brush your teeth.

9 | **Return to the party.**

How to Treat the Hiccups

Fill a tall glass with water. Holding the glass in front of you, lean forward over the glass so that your mouth is on the rim farthest away from you. Tilt the glass so that the bottom moves toward you and the top away from you; drink the water as it moves toward the front of the glass.

HOW TO TREAT FROSTBITE

Frostbite is a condition caused by the freezing of water molecules in skin cells and occurs in very cold temperatures. It is characterized by white, waxy skin that feels numb and hard. More severe cases result in a bluish black skin color, and the most severe cases result in gangrene, which may lead to amputation. Affected areas are generally fingertips and toes, and the nose, ears, and cheeks. Frostbite should be treated by a doctor. However, in an emergency, take the following steps.

1 Remove wet clothing and dress the area with warm, dry clothing.

2 Immerse frozen areas in warm water (100–105°F) or apply warm compresses for ten to thirty minutes.

3 If warm water is not available, wrap gently in warm blankets.

4 Avoid direct heat, including electric or gas fires, heating pads, and hot water bottles.

5 Never thaw the area if it is at risk of refreezing; this can cause severe tissue damage.

6 Do not rub frostbitten skin or rub snow on it.

7 Take a pain reliever such as aspirin or ibuprofen during rewarming to lessen the pain.
Rewarming will be accompanied by a severe burning sensation. There may be skin blistering and soft tissue swelling and the skin may turn red, blue, or purple in color. When skin is pink and no longer numb, the area is thawed.

8 Apply sterile dressings to the affected areas.
Place the dressing between fingers or toes if they have been affected. Try not to disturb any blisters, wrap rewarmed areas to prevent refreezing, and have the patient keep thawed areas as still as possible.

9 Get medical treatment as soon as possible.

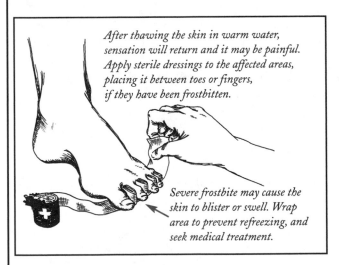

After thawing the skin in warm water, sensation will return and it may be painful. Apply sterile dressings to the affected areas, placing it between toes or fingers, if they have been frostbitten.

Severe frostbite may cause the skin to blister or swell. Wrap area to prevent refreezing, and seek medical treatment.

How to Treat Frostnip

Frostnip is the early warning sign of frostbite. Frostnip is characterized by numbness and a pale coloring of the affected areas. It can be safely treated at home.

1 Remove wet clothing.

2 Immerse or soak affected areas in warm water (100–105° F).

3 Do not allow patient to control water temperature—numb areas cannot feel heat and can be burned.

4 Continue treatment until skin is pink and sensation returns.

How to Avoid Frostbite and Frostnip

- Keep extremities warm and covered in cold weather.
- Use layered clothing and a face mask.
- Wear mittens instead of gloves, and keep the ears covered.
- Take regular breaks from the cold whenever possible to warm extremities.

HOW TO TREAT A TONGUE STUCK TO A POLE

1 Do not panic.

2 Do not pull the tongue from the pole.
Pulling sharply will be very painful.

3 Move closer to the pole.
Get as close as possible without letting more of the tongue's surface area touch the pole.

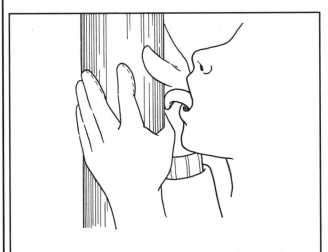

If your tongue is stuck to a pole, do not panic or pull it.
Warm the pole with your hands until your tongue comes loose.

4 | **Warm the pole with your hands.**
A tongue will stick when the surface of the pole is very cold. The top few layers of the tongue will freeze when the tongue touches the pole, causing bonding. Place your gloved hands on the area of the pole closest to the tongue. Hold them there for several minutes.

5 | **Take a test pull.**
As the pole warms, the frozen area around the tongue should begin to thaw. Gently pull the tongue away from the pole. You may leave a layer or two of skin on the pole, which will be painful, but the tongue will quickly heal.

Alternative Method

Use warm water.
Pour water from a water bottle over the tongue and the pole. Do not use water that is cold, or it may freeze and exacerbate the problem.

Be Aware

- Do not try to loosen your tongue with your own saliva: Although saliva is relatively warm, the small amount you will be able to generate is likely to freeze on your tongue.
- If another person is present, have him or her pour warm (not hot) water over your tongue. This may be difficult to articulate while your tongue is stuck—pantomiming a glass of water poured over your tongue should do the trick.

HOW TO DEAL WITH WEDDING-RELATED INJURIES

CAN'T FIT RING ON FINGER

★ **Try the other hand.**
The ring finger on the opposite hand may naturally be slightly smaller in diameter.

★ **Try a different finger.**
No one will notice if, for a little while, the ring is on the pinky.

★ **Elevate hand.**
Hands and feet swell in warm, humid weather. Hold your arm above your head for several minutes. Blood will flow from the hand and reduce the swelling so the ring will fit.

★ **Grease finger.**
Coat the ring finger with lip gloss, petroleum jelly, butter, margarine, or water.

★ **Cool finger.**
Submerge your ring finger in a glass of ice water for 15 minutes. The cold will constrict blood vessels and shrink the diameter of the finger slightly.

Elevate hand or soak ring finger in ice water to reduce swelling.

Foot Cut on Glass

1 Remove the shoe.
Unlace or unbuckle the shoe completely and remove it gently. If the victim is in severe pain, use scissors or a very sharp knife to cut the laces and save time.

2 Remove large shards of glass.
Wrap a napkin around the protruding piece. Using a single swift motion, pull the shard directly out of the foot.

3 Determine the source of bleeding.
Check for any remaining shards and remove them.

how to deal with wedding-related injuries

4 | **Stop the bleeding.**
Using towels, napkins, or tablecloths, apply direct pressure to the wound for 5 minutes. If the wound is spurting, sustain pressure for 15 minutes.

5 | **Clean the foot.**
Soak the foot in a bowl filled with warm water, then use a damp napkin or clean sponge to gently rub off any remaining blood.

6 | **Inspect the wound.**
Using your fingers, gently spread the sides of the wound apart. Look closely for any remaining glass shards. Remove with sterile tweezers (hold the tweezers under hot running water for 30 seconds, then in a candle flame for 30 seconds). The wound should stop bleeding profusely when all the glass has been removed.

7 | **Treat and bandage.**
Apply a thin layer of antibiotic ointment to the wound. Cover with a sterile adhesive bandage or gauze and medical tape.

Be Aware

- Wounds through the sole of the shoe may become infected by the microbe *Pseudomonas*.
- Wounds $1/2$ inch in length or longer should be sutured at a hospital.
- If the victim has not had a tetanus booster in the last five years, one should be given at a hospital within 48 hours of the injury.

- Seeping from the injury site may indicate that glass remains in the wound.
- When wrapping a glass in a napkin for the Jewish wedding ritual, be sure to lay the glass on its side before stomping on it.

Fall from Chair During Chair Dance

1 Seat the victim.
If the victim is conscious, move her to a chair and have her sit down. If she is unconscious on the floor, leave her in place. Most people who are knocked out after a fall regain consciousness within a few minutes.

2 Test cognition.
Ask the victim her name. Have her point to a few family members or friends in attendance and state their names. Ask her what type of event she is attending and the city in which it is being held. Ask her to state the date, including the day of the week and year. Correct answers indicate that she has not suffered a concussion. If she answers incorrectly, check again in 10 minutes.

3 Check responsiveness.
Ask the victim to follow your finger with her eyes as you move it from side to side and up and down. Ask her to move her arms and legs in coordinated motions. Help the victim stand, then ask her to walk forward, then backward, then forward again. Accomplishing these tasks indicates there is no neurological damage.

4 Watch for vomiting or loss of consciousness.
Pay particular attention to the victim for the next hour.

5 Prevent alcohol consumption.
Ask the victim if she has had anything alcoholic to drink or has taken tranquilizers or other medication, all of which may mimic the symptoms of injury. Do not let the victim drink.

Chapped Lips from Kissing

✪ Apply lip balm.
Spread a thin layer of petroleum jelly, vitamin E, or skin cream (used sparingly) to lips. Wait several minutes for the treatment to be absorbed.

✪ Apply olive oil.
Using your fingers, work a small amount of olive oil into your lips. Wait several minutes for the lips to become less slippery.

✪ Apply butter.
Work butter into your lips using your fingers. To prevent infection, avoid using butter if your lips are cracked and bleeding.

Kiss.

Apply.

Kiss.

how to deal with wedding-related injuries

HIT IN THE EYE WITH BOUQUET

1 | Check the eye for swelling.
If the eyelid is swollen shut and covering the eyeball, reduce the swelling before continuing with treatment. Place a handful of ice in a cloth napkin and twist it closed. Wrap it in a second napkin and place it on the injured eye for 15 minutes, removing it occasionally to check swelling.

2 | Examine the cornea.
Under a bright overhead light or pointing a flashlight at the injured eye, instruct the victim to look in all directions and blink repeatedly. Carefully examine the sclera (the white of the eye) and the cornea (the layer covering the pupil and iris) for any foreign material: petal shards, pieces of stem, or leaves.

3 | Assemble irrigation equipment.
Obtain a clean, unused liquor spout from the bartender. Place the pourer on a bottle of flat spring water or a bottle filled with cool tap water.

4 | Irrigate the cornea.
With the victim seated and her head tilted so she is looking up at the ceiling, gently push her eyelids back and away from the cornea using your thumb and forefinger. From a low height, delicately pour a steady stream of cool water on the eyeball. Occasionally wipe the area around the eye socket with a clean napkin.

5 Check the eye.
After a full bottle has been poured, dry the area and check the eyeball for remaining foreign material. If any material is still present, repeat irrigation with a second bottle of water.

6 Check for corneal abrasion.
Instruct the victim to look in all directions and blink repeatedly for several seconds. If she reports blurred vision, discomfort, or notes a sensation of something in her eye, a corneal abrasion may be present. Seek medical attention immediately.

SPRAINED ANKLE

1 Prepare a cold compress.
Place ice in a plastic bag. Wrap the bag in a piece of clothing, or place it in a second plastic bag.

2 Elevate the ankle.
Seat the victim and raise the injured ankle at least 18 inches from the ground; a chair works well. Keep the ankle in this position.

3 Hold the compress on the ankle.
The cold will constrict blood vessels and reduce swelling.

4 Leave the compress in place for 30 minutes.
If the sprain is particularly bad and swelling is rapid and severe, leave the compress on for 15 additional minutes.

5 | Test the ankle.
Have the victim put weight on the injured ankle. If standing or walking is still too painful, continue to step 6.

6 | Construct a pressure bandage.
Cut or tear a tablecloth, shirt, or another piece of material into two 3-foot-long, 4-inch-wide strips.

7 | Wrap the ankle.
Place one end of the bandage in the middle of the foot. Using a figure-8 pattern, bring the cloth up and over the ankle and back around the foot. The bandage should be snug and the ankle immobile. Use rubber bands, a garter, or two bow ties to secure the bandage to the leg.

8 | Administer pain medication.
Ibuprofen will reduce swelling and relieve pain. If ibuprofen is not available, offer acetaminophen or aspirin.

9 | Limit dancing.

How to See If You Have Lost Your Glasses

Draw 2 circles about the size of a pair of lenses on a piece of paper or cardboard. Use a pin or the tip of a sharp knife to poke at least a dozen small holes inside the circles. Hold the paper to your face and look through the holes.

CHAPTER 4
SOCIAL DISASTERS

HOW TO AVOID GOING TO THE WRONG COLLEGE

1 Visit the college during the school year on a day with a regular class schedule.

Visiting during holidays, homecoming, or other times when students are away or not in their normal routine will not give you an accurate picture of everyday life at the school.

2 Observe the students.
- Are the students walking energetically to class while talking animatedly, or are the few students in sight wandering aimlessly?
- Are the students bright-eyed, with glowing complexions, or are they red-eyed, with a pasty pallor?
- Are the students carrying armfuls of books and notebooks, or are they carrying surfboards and coolers?
- Are the students eagerly seeking out professors after class and in the cafeteria, or are the students ducking into doorways and under tables to avoid professors?
- Are students in class paying attention and taking notes, or are they wearing headphones, reading the newspaper, or dozing?

Compare the number of books in the library
to the number of seats in the stadium.

3 Evaluate the facilities and surroundings.
- Compare the number of books in the library to the number of seats in the stadium.
- Compare the number of flyers promoting free lectures to the number of flyers promoting spring break getaways.
- Compare the number of nearby art galleries to the number of nearby hair salons.
- Compare the number of nearby bookstores to the number of nearby bars.
- Compare the number of students wearing T-shirts with the school logo to the number of students not wearing any shirt.
- Compare the number of ads in the school newspaper offering "Students Available to Tutor" to the number of ads offering "Research Papers Written—Any Topic."
- Compare the number of times you hear chamber music to the number of times you hear sirens from emergency vehicles.

4 Select your school accordingly.

How to Identify a Party School

⭐ Assess the school's location.
Party schools are often those farthest from urban centers: Such a location necessitates that all social activities occur on campus or in campus-adjacent locations, and therefore there are parties daily due to the lack of other entertainment opportunities. Cities

with a warm climate and good beaches are also home to party schools, as many students opt for surfing, sunbathing, and pitchers of margaritas over class.

★ **Count the number of bars, liquor stores, fraternities, and sororities on or near campus.**
The more plentiful the watering holes and Greek organizations, the more likely the students are to party.

★ **Look for schools with successful sports teams.**
Schools with particularly winning sports programs are likely to offer many months of pre- and post-game victory parties. Avoid schools with losing records or sparsely attended games, and those with teams that usually lose the homecoming alumni game.

A warm climate often encourages a party atmosphere.

★ **Interview the school's administrators and alumni.**
Talk to the school's local boosters (ask the admissions office for names) about their memories of social activities at the school. If more than three of them recount stories of drinking at 6 A.M. or have no memory of college at all, the school is most likely a party school.

★ **Visit the school on a Thursday.**
A good party school will have multiple parties raging on this night. Walk the campus and listen carefully for whoops, yells, and loud music. Look for students staggering, talking loudly, or vomiting in the bushes, all of which are signs of raucous social activity. Enter a fraternity or sorority party. Gatherings without alcohol and centered around a knitting circle or a discussion of nineteenth-century English poetry indicate a college that does not measure up.

Interview the school's administrators.

HOW TO OPEN A BOTTLE WITHOUT AN OPENER

ANOTHER BOTTLE

1 Hold the bottle you wish to open upright in your nondominant hand.
Grip the neck of the target bottle, placing your index finger over the back edge of the cap.

2 Hold the second bottle horizontally around the label.
Grip this bottle, the opener, as though shaking hands with the bottle.

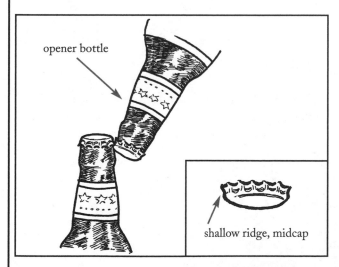

opener bottle

shallow ridge, midcap

3 Fit the shallow ridge found at midcap of the opener bottle under the bottom edge of the cap of the bottle you wish to open.
By using this ridge, and not the bottom of the cap, you will not risk opening the second bottle in step 4.

4 Using the opener bottle as a lever, press down and pry the cap off the target beer bottle.

5 Enjoy.

ALTERNATE METHOD:
Hold both bottles end to end perpendicular to the ground, with the crimped edges of the caps together, locking them in place. Pull. Be careful, however, as either or both bottle caps could come off.

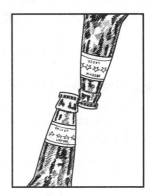

LIGHTER

1 Grip the bottle in your nondominant hand.
Make a fist around the top of the bottle so that your thumb overlaps your index finger and the web between your thumb and index finger sits in the groove under the cap.

2 Fit the bottom of the lighter under the teeth of the cap.
Position the lighter so that it rests on the middle knuckle of your index finger.

3 Press the top of the lighter down and toward the bottle.
Use the index finger on your dominant hand to provide resistance.

4 Pry off the cap.
If necessary, turn the bottle and repeat.

TABLE EDGE

1 Put the teeth of the bottle cap against the edge of a table.
The cap should be on top of the table edge; the bottle should be below the table. Do not attempt on a soft wood or antique table.

2 Use your fist to hit the bottle.
The bottle will take a downward trajectory, and the cap will pop off.

Screwdriver, Spoon, Fork, or Knife

1 Place the implement under the bottle cap, as high as it will go.

2 Pry off the cap.
Slowly go around the cap and lift up each crimped area with the tool, similar to opening a can of paint.

3 When the cap starts to move, fit the tool higher up under the cap and remove it.

Belt Buckle

1 Unfasten your belt buckle. If your pants are in danger of falling down, sit.

2 Pull the "tooth" of the buckle to one side.

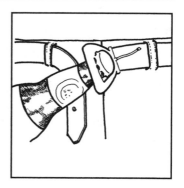

3 Fit the cap into the buckle so that one edge is wedged against the buckle.

4 Pry off.
Pull the bottle slowly. A quick tug may result in a spill.

5 Refasten your belt.

Deadbolt Lock

1 Fit your bottle into the lock. Place the head of the bottle into the recession in a doorframe into which a deadbolt slips, so that the cap fits against the notch in the lock's frame.

2 Pull up slowly. The bottle cap should pop right off.

Fire Hydrant

1 Look for an arrow on top of the hydrant labeled "open."

2 At the end of the arrow, locate the recess between the screw and the nut.

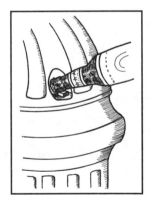

3 Insert the cap into the recess.

4 Press down slowly on the bottle until the cap comes off.

In-Line Skate

1 Place the cap between the shoe and the blade. Hold onto the bottle with your dominant hand. If you are wearing the skate, use the hand opposite the skate to open the bottle.

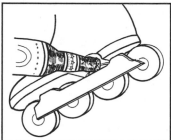

2 Pull up slowly on the bottle and pry off.
Quickly right the bottle to avoid spilling.

Metal Pool Bridge

1 Hold the stick of the bridge in one hand and a beer bottle in the other.
Do not attempt to open over the pool table.

2 Position the cap inside the opening of the bridge.
Fit the cap snugly against the edge.

3 Press down on the bottle. Slowly increase the pressure until the cap loosens. Right the bottle immediately to prevent spillage.

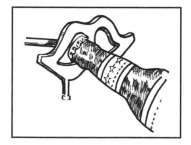

Vending Machine

1 Locate a newspaper, snack, or soda vending machine. An older soda machine might actually have a bottle opener.

2 Place the cap in the coin return.
Wedge the cap against the top of the opening.

3 Press down slowly until the cap is removed.

Be Aware
Never drink from a bottle with broken or chipped glass.

HOW TO
CARRY A DATE
WHO IS PASSED OUT

1 Plan to carry your date only for a short distance.
Your destination should be a nearby couch, taxi, or bed.
Do not attempt to carry him a long way.

2 Prepare to lift.
Bend your knees and place your stronger arm under your
date's back and the other under his knees. Your arms
should go all the way under and across his body.

3 Begin to lift your date.
Use the strength of your legs and knees, holding them
close to your body and keeping your back straight. Do not
lift with your back.

4 Stand up quickly.
In one continuous motion, rotate your date's body so that
your stronger arm guides him over your opposite shoulder.
The motion should be like tossing a sack of potatoes. His
upper body should be hanging over your back, his lower
body hanging over your front. Steady him with your other
hand.

5 Walk to your destination.

Place your stronger arm under your date's back.

Keep your back straight and lift with your knees.

Rotate your date's body over your opposite shoulder. The motion should be like tossing a sack of potatoes.

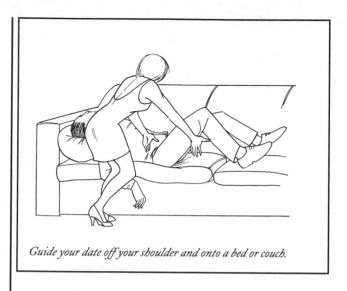

Guide your date off your shoulder and onto a bed or couch.

6 **Lower your date.**
Bending your knees and keeping your back straight, guide your date off your shoulder and onto a bed or couch or into a chair.

HOW TO SURVIVE IF YOU WAKE UP NEXT TO SOMEONE WHOSE NAME YOU DON'T REMEMBER

AT THEIR PLACE

1 Do not panic.
Evidence of your partner's name exists somewhere nearby. Your task will be to find it before she awakens, or before she starts any sort of meaningful conversation.

2 Get up and go to the bathroom.
The bathroom is a normal place to visit first thing in the morning, and it is also a place where you might discover her name.

3 Look through the medicine cabinet for prescription medicines with her name on the label.

4 Sort through magazines, looking for subscription labels with her name and address.

5 Go through a wastebasket to find discarded junk mail addressed to her.

*Look through medicine cabinets for prescription medicines with
your date's name on the label.*

6 | **Return to the bedroom.**

If she is awake, ask her to make coffee for you. Use the
time alone to search the bedroom for evidence. Look
for: wallet, checkbook, ID or name bracelet, photo
album, scrapbook, business cards (a stack of cards, not
just one), or luggage labels. If she is sleeping, look
for these and other items throughout the house.

Be Aware

Try to find at least two items with the same name to be certain that you have identified her, unless the name on one item rings a bell.

At Your Place

1 Use terms of endearment when addressing her.
Do not guess at her name. Acceptable terms of endearment are:
- Honey/Sweetie/Cutie
- Darling/Baby/Sugar
- Beautiful/Handsome/Gorgeous

2 Unless you are certain you have ample time, do not go through her belongings.
If your partner is showering, you can count on having at least a few minutes of privacy to search through her belongings. Otherwise, do not risk it—it would be far more embarrassing to be caught searching through her possessions than to admit you cannot remember her name. (She may be in the same predicament.)

3 Ask leading questions while making small talk.
Fishing for information is risky and can backfire by calling attention to what you are trying to do. However, if you feel you can pull it off, try to trick her into revealing her name:
- While getting dressed, pull out your own ID and ask her if she thinks that your hair is better now or in the picture. Laugh about how silly you used

how to survive if you wake up next to someone whose name you don't remember to look. Ask her if she likes the picture on her license. (She may think that you are checking her age.)

- Ask her if she ever had a nickname. She might say, "No, just [*Name*]."
- Ask her how she got her name.

4 As she is leaving, give her your business card and ask for hers.

If she does not have a business card, ask her to write her vital information on yours. Tell her you may want to send her a little surprise. Do not forget to send something later in the week and make sure that you spell her name correctly.

HOW TO DETERMINE IF YOUR DATE IS AN AXE MURDERER

1 Watch for the following:
- A Caucasian male in his twenties or thirties
- Obsession with fire or matches
- Cruelty to animals
- History of bed-wetting
- Sexually abused as a child
- Middle-class background combined with loner behavior
- Difficulty maintaining relationships

An individual who exhibits more than three of these traits may be dangerous.

2 Trust your intuition.
Your instinct is a powerful weapon. If something feels wrong, it probably is.

3 Check him out officially.
Obtain his social security number and investigate him. Call the Federal Prison Locator Service (202-307-3126) to determine if he was ever incarcerated. Many online companies can aid in financial reports or tracking down previous addresses. You may also want to enlist the services of a private detective.

how to determine if your date is an axe murderer

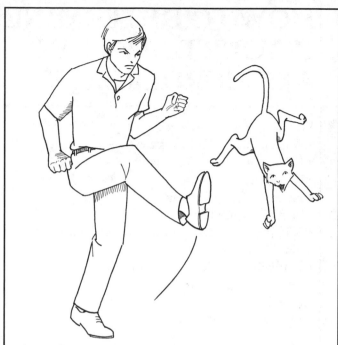

Axe murderers are usually Caucasian males in their twenties and thirties. They frequently behave cruelly toward animals and may also be obsessed with fire or matches.

4 **If you discover grounds for suspicion, break off the relationship immediately.**

Be clear and definite about your decision. Return all of his belongings and gifts. Do not make promises to keep in touch. Be straightforward and kind, and talk only about yourself and why the relationship no longer works for you. Do not blame him. Try not to make him angry.

5 Take steps to maintain your safety.
- Carry a cell phone.
- Install a home security system.
- Change your phone numbers.
- Stay near populated, well-lit areas.
- Apprise a friend or relative of your concerns.
- Document any strange or unusual happenings.
- Take a personal safety/self-defense class.

HOW TO DETERMINE THE GENDER OF YOUR DATE

1 Look at her (or his) hand.
Compare the length of your date's fourth and second fingers. Most men have ring fingers that are conspicuously longer than their index fingers, whereas most women have ring fingers that are close to the same length. Testosterone levels likely account for the greater length.

Also take notice of the amount of hair on your date's knuckles, hands, and forearms. Most men will have visible, dark hair (or signs of recently removed hair) on their hands and wrists, and sometimes knuckles.

2 Be suspicious of baggy clothing.
Your date may be trying to conceal a telltale bulge.

3 Look for an Adam's apple.
Most men have a bump in the middle of their throat. Most women do not.

Compare shoulders and hips

Watch for swaying

Men's shoulders tend to be broader than their hips, while women's hips and shoulders tend to be closer to the same width. When ascending stairs, women tend to sway more than men.

4 | Observe shoulders and hips.
Men's shoulders tend to be broader than their hips, while women's hips and shoulders tend to be closer to the same width. Do not be fooled by shoulder pads.

5 | Follow your date up a flight of stairs.
Take note of how she (or he) moves while ascending. Men tend to walk in a more "straight ahead" motion with minimal "wobbling" back and forth. Women tend to sway a bit from side to side, due to the position of their pelvises. Women also tend to lean forward slightly.

Be Aware

- Look for at least three of these characteristics before you draw conclusions about your date's gender, then make your plans accordingly.
- Voice is not always a good indicator of gender—a low voice may simply be the result of hard living.

HOW TO FEND OFF
A PICKUP ARTIST

1 Recognize the traits of a pickup artist.
Is your suitor overly charming and quick with cash?
Does he appear to have an immediate connection
with you? Is he scanning the room while talking to
you? Is he calling you familiar or condescending
names such as "honey," "sweetie," or "babe"?

2 Do not accept drinks.
Letting a pickup artist buy you drinks will encourage
him and make him feel he is entitled to your attentions.

3 Keep personal information to yourself.
Do not give him your name, and do not tell him
where you live, who you are waiting for, or any other
detail or insight into your personal life or plans.

4 Make it clear that you are not interested.
Be direct and forceful. If he persists, you may have to
become rude or leave. If you make it obvious that
nothing is going to happen that evening, he'll move
on to other prospects.

5 Turn away and ignore him.
Talk to a friend or the person sitting on the other side
of you. The pickup artist likes the chase most of all—
put a stop to the chase and he will look elsewhere.

The Elbow Knock: Turn back to glance at the pickup artist and sweep your elbow toward the glass.

The Time Check: Turn your wrist to look at your watch, and spill your drink on the pickup artist.

6 Cause an "accident."

- The Elbow Knock: Use this technique if you are seated at a bar or table. Notice where glasses and plates are located on your table. Turn around to talk to a friend, or simply look away, and position your elbow. As you turn back, sweep your elbow into any glasses or plates on the table, knocking them into his lap or onto his shirt.

- The Hair Flip: While standing facing your suitor, bring your hand up to adjust your hair. Do this quickly so that he tips his glass toward his body and his drink spills all over him.

- The Time Check: While standing next to your would-be suitor, hold your drink in the hand of your watch arm. Say, "Is it *time* yet?" Then turn your wrist to look at your watch, thereby spilling the drink on the pickup artist.

7 Apologize insincerely.

HOW TO SAVE YOUR DATE FROM CHOKING

1 Speak firmly.
Keep your voice low and your sentences short. All communications should be in the imperative. Explain that you are going to perform the Heimlich maneuver.

2 Tell your date to stand up and stay put.

3 Hug your date from behind.
Put your arms around your date and make one hand into a fist.

4 Place your fist in your date's solar plexus.
The solar plexus is the first soft spot in the center of the body, between the navel and the ribs.

5 Place your other hand, palm open, over your fist.

6 Tell your date to bend forward slightly.
If your date does not respond, push on the upper back and repeat, "Lean forward."

7 Pull your fist in and up.
Use force and a quick motion. This will push out the residual lung gas under pressure, clearing any obstructions from the trachea.

chapter 4: social disasters

8 Repeat steps 3 through 7 several times if choking persists.

9 After several unsuccessful attempts, instruct your date to bend over the back of a chair.
The top of the chair should be at the level of your date's hips.

Pull your fist in and up, quickly and with strength.

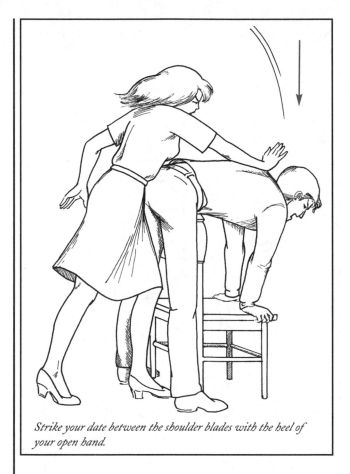

Strike your date between the shoulder blades with the heel of your open hand.

10 Strike your date between the shoulder blades with the heel of your open hand.
The blow generates gaseous pressure in a blocked airway and, with a head-down position, sometimes works when the Heimlich does not.

Be Aware

- If the choking is noiseless—or if your date raises her hands to her throat—then the air passage may be completely blocked and you must proceed quickly.
- If your date is coughing or gagging, you simply need to be polite, smile sympathetically, and offer water when the choking is over. Water does nothing for choking, but it gives the choker some time to regain dignity.
- In most cases, the first thrust of the Heimlich maneuver will dislodge the choked item from the trachea. Once the choking is over, your date will need some time to recover: a sip of brandy, a quiet moment. Do not rush your date to the emergency room; in most cases, there is no need to go to the hospital after the blockage has been removed.

HOW TO SURVIVE
IF YOU HAVE
EXCESSIVE GAS

1 Limit your lactose intake during a date.
Many people suffer from an inability to digest milk sugar, or lactose. Colon bacteria ferment the milk sugar, forming a gas that creates a bloated feeling. Keep your intake to less than half a cup at a sitting, and avoid dairy products before your date.

2 Eat a small meal.
Eating a huge dinner on a date is a sure-fire way to precipitate gas.

3 Avoid gas-forming foods.
Bacteria ferment the indigestible carbohydrates in beans, broccoli, cabbage, and other vegetables and fruits into gases.

4 Drink peppermint tea.
Replace an after-dinner drink with a cup or two of peppermint tea. This herb may give you some relief from the gas discomfort that follows a meal.

5 Emit the gas in private.
As a last resort, head to the bathroom. If you feel bloated but are unable to pass gas easily, you can facilitate the emission of gas as follows:

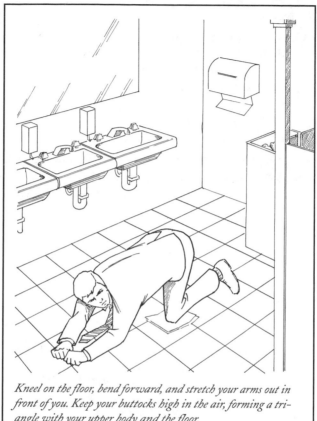

Kneel on the floor, bend forward, and stretch your arms out in front of you. Keep your buttocks high in the air, forming a triangle with your upper body and the floor.

Place paper towels on the floor. Kneel on the towels, bend forward to the floor, and stretch your arms out in front of you. Keep your buttocks high in the air, forming a triangle with your upper body and the floor. This position will force out the unwanted gas and relieve the pressure.

Be Aware

- On average, humans produce ¾ of a liter of gas daily, which is released 11 to 14 times a day.
- Men typically produce more gas than women because they consume more food.

GASSY FOODS TO AVOID

No two digestive systems are alike. Experiment with foods to determine which ones affect you most. In the meantime, exercise caution around the following high-risk items:

- Beans (particularly baked beans)
- Borscht
- Broccoli
- Brussels sprouts
- Cabbage
- Carbonated beverages
- Cauliflower
- Chili
- Cucumbers
- Fatty foods
- Fresh fruit
- Grains and fiber, especially pumpernickel bread
- Gum
- Onions
- Oysters
- Salads (green)

HOW TO SURVIVE
A WORKPLACE
ROMANCE

★ **Do not tell colleagues.**
Do not discuss any aspect of your relationship with anyone at work, even close friends. Avoid telltale references, such as, "When we were at the movies last night . . . " Do not play guessing games with co-workers, such as, "I'm going out with someone from the office but you'll never guess who."

★ **Resist physical contact at the office.**
Avoid all physical contact, including kissing, handholding, hugging, casual touching, and back rubs, even if you think you are alone. Maintain at least a foot of personal space between you and the person you are dating.

★ **Send gifts to the home.**
Do not have flowers, candy, clothing, or other personal items sent to the office, even with an unsigned card: People will begin asking questions.

★ **Do not use company e-mail to send personal notes.**
Many employers monitor e-mail messages, and even deleted messages are stored. It is also too easy to send an e-mail to the wrong person or to "everyone."

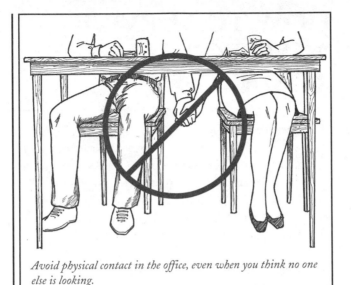

Avoid physical contact in the office, even when you think no one else is looking.

⭐ **Avoid long or excessive lunch dates.**
While it is acceptable for colleagues to eat together, extended or repeated outings may attract notice. Maintain the lunch routine you practiced before you started dating your co-worker.

⭐ **Avoid arriving and departing together.**
Unless you are in a car pool with others, stagger your arrival and departure times.

⭐ **Use discretion.**
At company picnics or parties, or at off-site meetings, do not drink excessively, dance intimately, or openly display affection with your office significant other.

Be Aware
- Most office romances begin in the spring.
- Dating more than one person from the same company at the same time is not a good idea.

The Break-Up

⭐ **Do not break up at work.**
Emotions can be difficult to hide, and people can act irrationally when they are upset. The workplace, especially in a cubicle but even in a private office, is a poor choice of location for a confrontation. Avoid breaking up over lunch hour, as well.

⭐ **Break up over a long weekend.**
Choose a time when your partner will have several days to heal before having to see you at the office. Try to be sensitive to his or her feelings, however: Do not break up just before the other person leaves on an extended vacation.

⭐ **Be prepared for the worst.**
A bad break-up may require you to transfer or even resign, particularly if you are dating someone above you in the office hierarchy. Ending a relationship with someone who reports to you could lead to a charge of sexual discrimination.

★ Do not immediately begin dating someone else at work.
Your new relationship may be hurtful to your ex, if you are spotted. You may also gain a reputation for being opportunistic or desperate.

★ Do not discuss personal feelings or emotions with your ex while at work.
If you want to check on how your former lover is doing, call at home.

Be Aware
No matter what you call it—fishing off the company pier, mentoring the intern, kissing company cousins, refilling the toner, mergers and acquisitions—office romances are dangerous.

HOW TO
SURVIVE MEETING
THE PARENTS

1 Pay attention to your surroundings.
If you are prone to spilling things or tripping over rugs, move slowly and carefully. Present an image of confidence and poise.

2 Greet them with a firm, but brief, handshake.
A weak handshake is a turnoff, but so is squeezing too hard. Shake hands so that the entire hand is clasped. Let go of the hand after a few pumps. Maintain eye contact.

3 Do not kiss or hug the parents unless they make the first move.
If they offer air kisses, fine, but never kiss a potential in-law on the mouth. If they opt to hug you, do not retreat from it.

4 Call them "Mr." and "Mrs." unless they ask you to address them by their first names.
This shows respect. Do not shorten or change their names or call them "Mom" or "Dad."

5 Give them personal space.
Allow at least three feet of space between you during conversation.

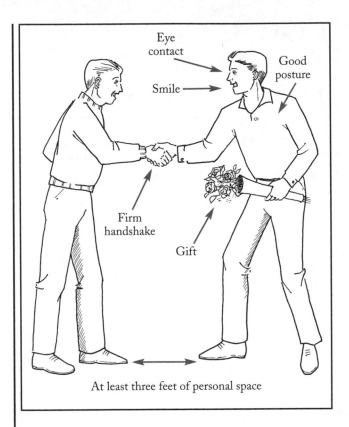

Eye contact

Smile

Good posture

Firm handshake

Gift

At least three feet of personal space

6 Show poise.

Be positive, good natured, and relaxed. Smile, but not continuously: if you look happy all of the time, something's not right. Remember that good posture projects confidence and successfulness. Walk, stand, and sit up straight. Speak loud enough to be heard.

7 | Be sincere and be yourself.
Do not pretend to be someone you are not. People can spot a fake a mile away. Do not try too hard to make an impression. At the same time, do not act too familiar—no winking, shoulder punching, or joking. Follow their lead.

8 | Send a note or card the next day.
Mention how nice it was to finally meet them and that you look forward to seeing them again. If you stayed at their house for a while, thank them for an enjoyable visit.

Be Aware
Practicing the following social graces can help make a favorable impression:
- Ring the doorbell once only. Do not lean on the bell or pound the door.
- Turn off your cell phone and pager.
- If invited to dinner, bring wine, flowers, or dessert, even if they say not to.
- Wait to be invited inside, and wait to be seated. Do not sit down before they do.
- Pet the dog or cat.
- Compliment them on only one or two things: the view, the couch, a painting, the flowers—don't overdo it.
- Do not spend too much time in the bathroom (and do not go too often).

HOW TO RAISE MONEY FOR YOUR WEDDING

⭐ **Ask family members to pay for specific expenses.**
Have numbers ready to justify costs. If you sense resistance, threaten to elope or to have the reception at a seedy nightclub. For grandparents, offer upgrades at the reception in exchange for funding, such as seating at a table far from the band, their food served first, or wider cushioned seats.

⭐ **Register for wedding ceremony and reception components.**
Instead of a bridal registry for china, crystal, and silver, register for floral arrangements, liquor for the reception, the band, limousine service, and each course of the meal.

⭐ **Hold a raffle.**
Offer the guests a chance to buy tickets to win the wedding dress, a ride in the limo, or a chance to join the honeymoon.

⭐ **Wash guests' cars.**
Hire a student at a low hourly rate to sell expensive car washes to the guests as they attend the ceremony and reception.

Procure sponsors to help defray costs.

★ **Sell your belongings on Internet auction sites.**
Check to see which items you've registered for have been bought, or estimate which items you are sure to receive, and sell them online. The buyer will send payment, and, after the wedding, you send the sold item.

★ **Procure sponsors.**
Strike a deal with a local company. Agree to place its logo on the invitation, wedding dress, tuxedo, or cake. Have the band leader announce each song with, "This song has been brought to you by the good people at *[name of company]*." Hang company banners around the altar and behind the bandstand. Allow the company to set up a kiosk at the ceremony and reception site to dispense information, key chains, and other swag.

★ **Sell incentive packages to investors.**
Offer a percentage of wedding gifts, naming rights to kids, occasional dinners at your home, an invitation to the wedding (with preferred seating), the first dance with the bride/groom, and, for enough money, the opportunity to give away the bride.

HOW TO MAINTAIN COMPOSURE DURING A WEDDING CEREMONY

CRYING JAG

⭐ Take deep, measured breaths.
Inhale through your nose and exhale through your mouth. Deep breathing will calm you and prevent hyperventilation brought on by crying.

⭐ Stare at inanimate objects.
Focus on floral arrangements, your clothing, or the floor.

⭐ Recall trivial details.
Try to remember the color of your childhood blanket, or the make and model of all the cars you have owned. Attempt to say the alphabet or the months of the year backward.

⭐ Stand up straight.
Crying will cause you to bend forward and make your head and shoulders shake. Concentrate on good posture: Keep your back straight and your head held high to combat the physical effects of your emotions.

Be Aware

Crying at weddings tends to be contagious and mutually reinforcing. Do not look at others who are crying or you may lose control.

LAUGHING FIT

⭐ **Bite your tongue.**
Bite down on your tongue hard enough to cause pain but not so hard that you cause bleeding or other injury.

⭐ **Prick your finger.**
Using the pin from your boutonniere or a thorn from a rose in your bouquet, quickly stick the pad of your thumb to cause pain. Put pressure on the pricked area for several minutes to avoid bloodstained clothing.

⭐ **Pinch yourself.**
The skin on the back of the upper arm is very sensitive. Squeeze a small section of skin between the thumb and index finger of your opposite hand. Release quickly to avoid a bruise.

⭐ **Think about how much the wedding costs.**

HICCUPS

1 **Inhale through your mouth.**

2 **Hold your breath.**

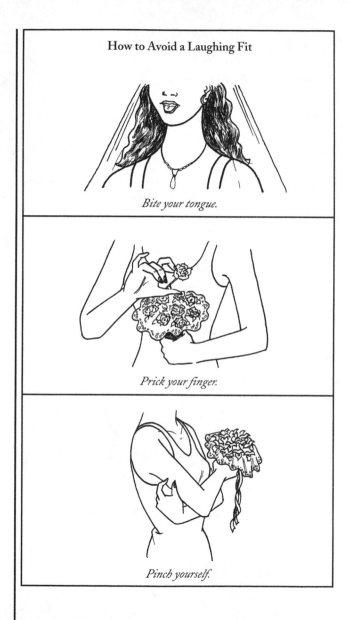

How to Avoid a Laughing Fit

Bite your tongue.

Prick your finger.

Pinch yourself.

3 | Slowly count to ten.

4 | Swallow three times slowly.

5 | Exhale.

6 | Repeat.

Standing on your head while drinking backward from a glass will not cure hiccups.

Be Aware

Swallow a flat (nonheaping) teaspoon or one paper packet of sugar in one quick gulp. Do not use a sugar substitute. Do not use salt.

FLATULENCE

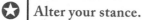 **Alter your stance.**
Flatulence is more audible with the legs and buttocks close together. Shift your position so your feet are approximately 3 feet apart.

Sit down.

Shift the blame.
Look disapprovingly at a nearby guest or member of the bridal party. Do not look accusingly at your betrothed.

Be Aware

- Avoid introducing excess gas into your system. Do not smoke, chew gum, or drink carbonated beverages, and avoid beans, broccoli, cabbage, cauliflower, onions, and dairy products (if lactose intolerant) just before the ceremony.
- Chew activated charcoal tablets before the wedding. The charcoal will absorb odor caused by intestinal bacteria. Do not chew briquettes.

how to maintain composure during a wedding ceremony

HOW TO REPAIR A DROPPED CAKE

Minor Shifting or Smashed Frosting

1 Smooth out rough edges with confectioners' sugar or chopped coconut.

2 Reconstruct with icing or whipped cream.
Damaged portions of a white cake may be built up and out using small amounts of buttercream or whipped cream. Apply with a spoon or butter knife. For a cake with chocolate frosting, mix slightly melted chocolate with confectioners' sugar to form a paste, then spread over the damaged area and cover as above.

3 Hide damage to the side of the cake with paper doilies.
Cut several long strips from a paper doily: The strips should match the height of the damaged layer. If necessary, use clear tape on the side that will be touching the cake to connect multiple sections. Wrap the doily around the layer and secure with small dabs of frosting. Remove the doily before serving.

4 Use fruit or nonpoisonous flowers to hide repairs.
Roses, pansies, and daisies are all nontoxic and attractive. Avoid lilies of the valley, calla lilies, and wisteria, all of which are poisonous. Place two or three large

chapter 4: social disasters

strawberries over damaged areas, with several others around the cake to visually balance the repair.

Major Damage

1 | Set aside any undamaged layers from the dropped cake.

2 | Replace damaged layers.
Depending on the shape of the cake, locate rect-angular or round boxes that approximately match the size of the damaged layers. Hat boxes work well for round cakes.

3 | Place real cake layers on box layers.

4 | Poke wooden skewers or thin dowel rods through all the layers.
Cover holes with frosting. The rods will prevent the layers from sliding, especially in warm weather.

5 | Cover exposed sections of boxes with frosting as you would an actual cake.
Add flowers or other flourishes to match the existing cake.

6 | Prepare to move the cake directly after cutting.
Once the first cut has been made, the cake should be taken immediately into the kitchen and the real layers sliced sparingly.

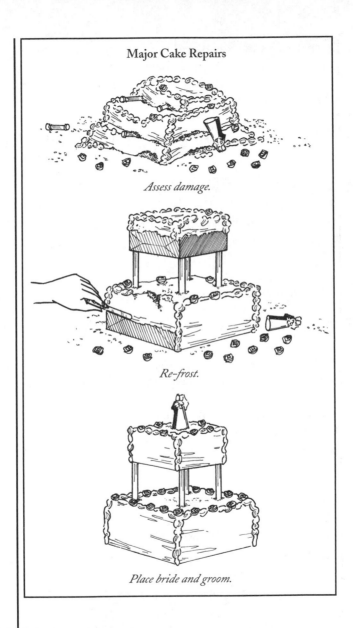

Major Cake Repairs

Assess damage.

Re-frost.

Place bride and groom.

Be Aware

- If the top layer of a tiered cake is damaged beyond repair, completely remove it and all support pillars, then repair remaining sections, making the next-to-the-top layer the top.
- If time permits, the caterer or pastry chef could bake or purchase a last-minute sheet cake. Serve that instead.

HOW TO DEAL WITH A SCREAMING BABY ON AN AIRPLANE

1   Make highly visible efforts to quiet your child.
Passengers and flight attendants will not be as upset with you if they think that you are doing everything you can. Talk to your child, sing to him, and bounce him; offer him a bottle, pacifier, or food; rock him; walk him up and down the aisles; distract him with the air safety card, airsickness bags, or in-flight phone. Do everything you can think of to calm your baby, and do it loudly and noticeably.

2   Create confusion and distraction.
If your child has not quieted down, act crazy. Cross your eyes; make the "beebeebeebeebeebeebeebee" sound by moving your finger up and down between your lips; sing, preferably an aria, at full volume—do anything you can to distract your child from his tantrum. Then soothe him using more traditional methods.

3   Do not panic if your child will still not calm down.
Remember that this is only a moment in time, and that no matter how many nasty looks you are getting from fellow passengers, you are doing the best you can.

Tell yourself you will never see these people again.

4 **Use drugs and alcohol.**
Certain over-the-counter drugs can be administered in an emergency situation. Cold or allergy medicine for children, in particular, works well and usually causes drowsiness and a calming feeling. However, the medication may take half an hour or longer to take effect, and it frequently produces the opposite effect on children, speeding them up. The alcohol is for your consumption, in appropriate doses.

5 **Use the lavatory.**
If your child still will not calm down, retreat to the lavatory with him until he exhausts himself. Hold the baby in front of the mirror and say, "There's another baby in the room!" or pretend that you are "walking downstairs" by moving back and forth in the lavatory, stooping lower with each step.

6 | Bribe fellow passengers for forgiveness.
Offer free drinks, extra bags of snacks, earplugs, and reimbursement for dry-cleaning expenses.

7 | Remind yourself that you will never see these people again.
Repeat.

Be Aware
- First-class and business-class passengers usually have less tolerance for screaming babies.
- Do not pretend you do not know the child. Laws regarding child abandonment and neglect are more troublesome than annoyed passengers.

IF YOU ARE OUT OF DIAPERS

1 | Ask the flight attendant for several cloth napkins.
Cloth napkins make an excellent temporary diaper.

2 | Fold two cloth napkins into rectangles.

3 | Place the two folded napkins (the liner) in the center of a third cloth napkin (the diaper).

4 | Secure as you would a normal cloth diaper.
Effective fasteners include safety pins, bobby pins, hair clips, or butterfly-style binder clips. Use for short periods only, since the starch in the napkins may irritate the baby's skin.

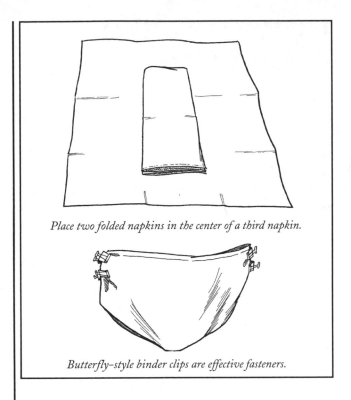

Place two folded napkins in the center of a third napkin.

Butterfly-style binder clips are effective fasteners.

Be Aware

The following items should not be used in place of a diaper:

- Silk scarf
- Wool blanket
- Suede jacket
- Baseball cap
- Straw hat
- Flotation device

HOW TO SURVIVE A FAMILY CAR TRIP

1 Line the seats with a large bath towel or sheet.
The cover will protect the back seat and expedite cleanup later.

2 Leave early.
Start a long trip early—before dawn—to assure that kids will be sleepy and will nap for the first few hours of the ride. If they awaken at or near rush hour, pull over to avoid traffic and get a break from driving.

Bring only what you really need.

3 | Bring along a few key items, but only what you really need.
Essential items include snacks, games, open-ended creative toys, and passive entertainment devices (such as CD players and portable DVD players).

4 | Make frequent stops.
Do not expect small children to sit still for more than an hour or two at a time. Make frequent rest stops to switch drivers, stretch, throw a ball, run around, and use the bathroom. These stops also serve to fend off carsickness and keep the driver alert.

How to Pee at the Side of the Road

1 | Pull over.
Find a spot with adequate coverage, usually in the form of bushes or thick trees, that is a safe distance from the road.

2 | Exit the car away from the road.
Leave the door open to further block visibility. Take tissues or napkins with you, if available.

3 | Select a position behind a tree or bush.
Position your child 180 degrees from view of oncoming traffic. In general, boys should pee facing downhill, while girls should pee facing uphill.

how to survive a family car trip

4 | **Assess the weather conditions.**
Assess the direction of the wind, and position your child to pee with it.

5 | **Assemble a "human shield."**
If there is little or no coverage, line up other members of the family to form a "human shield."

6 | **Keep quiet.**
Do not speak to the family member who is attempting to go. It may be distracting and will only prolong the stop and the trip.

child answering nature's call

HOW TO IDENTIFY A NIGHTMARE WORKPLACE

1 | Interview at the beginning or end of the day.
Arrive early for your morning interview and observe the workers as they arrive. Slouching, pouting, and dejected expressions indicate low morale. Note whether workers acknowledge the receptionist with a smile and a greeting or are oblivious to the receptionist. With an interview at the end of the day, observe if large numbers of workers leave promptly at quitting time, which may indicate a bored, clock-watching staff. Large numbers of people working late, however, may indicate that employees are overworked and deadlines are unrealistic.

2 | Examine the bathrooms.
Are the bathrooms clean? Is there enough toilet paper? Are paper towels strewn about the floor? Lack of attention to these small details may indicate a lack of respect for the workplace and lack of attention to larger details.

3 | Monitor the air quality.
Does the work area have natural light and outside air? Is the environment quiet? Is the air too hot or too cold? Are there any rancid or chemical smells? Is smoke billowing from any vents or machinery? Are

Signs of a Troubled Workplace

slouching and pouting

staff leaves promptly at quitting time

workers sniffing or sneezing frequently? All of these are indicators of poor air quality or a "sick" workplace.

4 Look for signs of a troubled workplace.
- Lack of personal photos on desks—only motivational images of rowers and bears catching salmon
- Droopy eyelids obscuring the whites of the workers' eyes
- Multiple sandwiches (partially eaten) and cans of soda at workstations
- Employees sleeping, doodling, or fist-fighting at meetings
- Employees with their foreheads on their desks, fists pounding the desktops
- Outdated or no-longer-manufactured candy in the vending machine
- Brown water in the cooler
- Flickering or humming fluorescent lights
- Music playing through speakers in the ceiling
- "Warning: Hazardous Waste" signs
- Groups of workers whispering
- Individual workers whispering to themselves
- Groups of workers silently praying
- Office layout based on slave ship rather than feng shui
- Carpet stains that could be coffee, could be blood

If you observe three or more of the above danger signs, you may have discovered a nightmare workplace.

5 Evaluate.
Is this the job for you?

HOW TO GET A JOB YOU'RE NOT QUALIFIED FOR

FANCY RESTAURANT

Restaurant interviews focus on your service experience, knowledge of standard service customs and procedures, and familiarity with a wide range of food items. You also are judged on your overall appearance and general demeanor.

ATTIRE
Wear:
- Tuxedo

or

- White blouse with black skirt (below the knee)

Do Not Wear:
- Ripped jeans
- Facial hair (except a groomed mustache)
- Dark-colored nail polish
- Lots of jewelry (limit is a watch, a wedding band and/or engagement ring, and a pair of stud earrings)

PARAPHERNALIA TO BRING
- Table crumber
- Worm (waiter's corkscrew)
- Matches or a lighter

- Cover (one person's dinner—derives from a single dinner plate with metal cover)
- Gooseneck (gravy boat)
- Eighty-sixed (the item is gone/finished)
- Bring-back (an unsatisfactory dish returned to the kitchen)
- Weeded (when you are attempting to serve too many tables at once)
- One fancy French wine appellation, perfectly pronounced

CRITICAL KNOWLEDGE
- American banquet trays should be carried in the left hand, leaving the right hand free to pick up service items and open doors. (Doors in restaurants in the United States swing out and have hinges on the right.) Your left hand should be flat, palm up, thumb toward your body, under the center of the bus tray, with the tray resting on your shoulder.
- You should be able to carry 10 covers at once.
- Stack the covers on the banquet tray as follows: One stack of two plates at each oblong end of the tray, one stack of three plates directly over your left shoulder, and one stack of three plates just beyond it.
- Hold cocktail trays at waist level, for beverages.
- Never put empty dishes and glassware together on the same banquet tray.

- Serve food from the left, drinks from the right. In the United States, all food items should be served from the left, using the left hand, left foot in toward the table. Drinks should be poured and items cleared from the right, using the right hand, right foot in. (French restaurants and exclusive hotels may use "modern French service," with all items served and cleared from the right.)
- Do not look at drinks as you carry them on a tray—it is easier to maintain a steady hand if you are not watching the liquids shift.
- Offer job references from out-of-town restaurants. Say, "I worked for years at Chez Louis in Chicago." If pressed for the name of a person, add, "Unfortunately, the restaurant never reopened after the fire and I don't know how to reach the owner/manager anymore."

CEO

Applying for a CEO job is a lengthy process and will require multiple interviews. Be prepared for several face-to-face meetings with the human resources department, senior management, and board members.

ATTIRE
Wear:
- Navy or beige suit, white shirt, and a solid or wide-striped tie
  or

- Navy or beige jacket and skirt or a pantsuit or dress (for less conservative companies)
- Expensive-looking watch
- Shined shoes

Do Not Wear:
- Bow tie or clip-on necktie
- Loud-print blouse
- Open-toed shoes
- Pastels

Do Not:
- Remove your jacket during the interview
- Have dirty fingernails

Paraphernalia to Bring
- Leather portfolio
- Ultra-expensive fountain pen
- Cigar clipper
- Putter (collapsible)
- Credit cards and large bills—no coins or bills smaller than $20

Buzzwords to Use
- Gross margin (the difference between sales revenue and the cost of the goods sold)
- Book value (the value of all the assets)
- EBITDA (earnings before interest, taxes, depreciation, and amortization)
- Buy-in
- Buy-out

how to get a job you're not qualified for

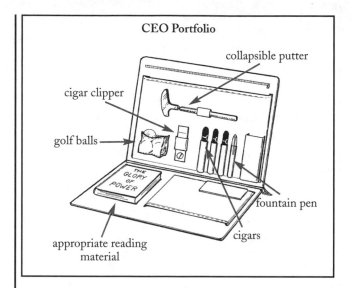

CEO Portfolio

collapsible putter

cigar clipper

golf balls

THE GLORY OF POWER

fountain pen

appropriate reading material

cigars

- Re-conceptualize
- Re-energize
- Right-size

CRITICAL KNOWLEDGE

- Ask about the company's challenges over the next 6 to 12 months, its business plan or model, and whether it is in "growth" mode.
- Focus your questions on the business as a whole, the marketplace, or the global economy rather than on the details of the job.
- To prepare, read books on good grammar and writing style rather than business books. People are always more impressed with someone who communicates clearly, effectively, and correctly.

Use spell-checking software whenever you draft a cover letter or resume.

Insider Tip

- Be sure to ask about the number of stock options available to you, as well as their "strike price" (the price at which you can exercise them).
- When asked about your hiring strategy, say, "To hire people smarter than I am." Presidents like hearing this—it makes them trust you.
- Always negotiate for a higher salary and better benefits than offered—presidents will be more comfortable placing the business in the hands of a bulldog.

Forklift Operator

Driving a forklift requires specialized skills and lots of practice, so mention that you have operated a "fork" or "stacker" at many previous job sites.

Attire

Wear:
- Clean T-shirt
- Work boots
- Baseball cap

Do Not Wear:
- Loafers or flip-flops
- Necktie
- Collared shirts other than flannel
- Short pants

how to get a job you're not qualified for

Paraphernalia to Bring
- Lunch box/cooler
- Work gloves
- Cigarettes or chew
- Multipurpose tool on belt

Buzzwords to Use
- Towmotor, high-low, stacker, truck (slang fork-lift names)
- Forks, carriage, mast/upright, load backrest (important parts of the forklift)
- Cage/DOG (for Driver's Overhead Guard)/ ROPS (pronounced "ropes," Roll-Over Protection Structure)

Critical Knowledge
- The primary fork controls on a forklift are the lift-lower, the tilt forward-back, and the side shifter.
- A fork has a transmission selector (forward, reverse, neutral), steering wheel, parking brake, and accelerator and brake pedals. Most units are now automatic, and these may also have a separate inching pedal to the left of the brake pedal that slips the transmission and moves the forklift very slowly. The inching pedal may also be built into the brake pedal itself: Depress it slowly for inching, fully for braking.

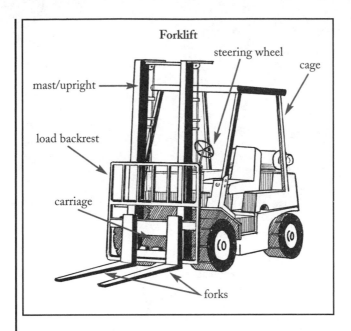

Forklift

steering wheel

cage

mast/upright

load backrest

carriage

forks

INSIDER TIP

- Mention that you have handled concrete blocks and paper rolls. Add that you have used 2,000- to 10,000-pound units (these refer to the forklift's lifting capacity, not the weight of the unit itself), as well as units equipped with paper-roll clamps. You might also say that you've handled "your fair share" of four-wheel sit-downs, walk-behinds, and pallet trucks.

- Ask about the number of trailers and the number of pallets you will be expected to handle per day (fewer is better).

- Since most people who operate forklifts are not licensed to do so, don't worry that you do not have a license to show.

Brain Surgeon

Brain surgeons train for as long as eight years after medical school, so you should be, or appear to be, at least 34.

Attire
Wear:
- Suit and tie

or

- Blouse and skirt

Do Not Wear:
- White lab coat or scrubs
- Stethoscope around your neck

Paraphernalia to Bring
- Surgical loupe. Loupes are worn like glasses or over glasses and provide strong magnification during surgery. They are custom-fitted and all brain surgeons have them. Borrow a pair, or carry an empty loupe case. The case should be wooden with a surgeon's name engraved on a metal template. Keep the name on the template obscured. If you cannot borrow an actual loupe or case, substitute a wood case about 10 inches long by 5 inches wide. Do not wear surgical loupes on a chain around your neck, as you would reading glasses or sunglasses.
- Do not carry other surgical instruments.
- Do not carry medical charts.

chapter 4: social disasters

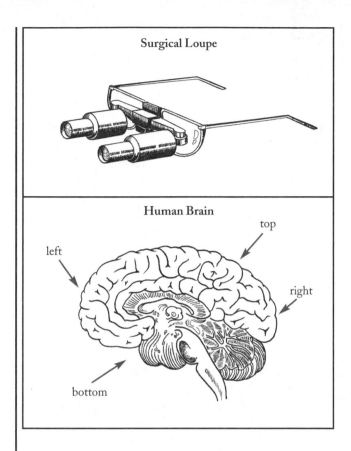

Surgical Loupe

Human Brain

top

left

right

bottom

Buzzwords to Use
- Surgical drill (for drilling into bone)
- Deep brain stimulation (abbreviated DBS, targets particular areas of the brain with electrical pulses)
- Spinal instrumentation (implantation of permanent therapeutic devices in the spine)

how to get a job you're not qualified for

- Ask about the hospital's type of operating micro-scope and its image-guidance system. Also ask about the strength of the magnet in the hospital's MRI (magnetic resonance imager).
- All brain surgery begins with either drilling or sawing through the cranium.

INSIDER TIP
- Interviewers will want to know about papers you have published in well-known medical journals. Mention that you are awaiting publication in *Neurosurgery* (frequently called the "red journal"), the *Journal of Neurosurgery* (known as the "white journal"), and are expecting a book contract.

SHOE SALESPERSON

Shoe sales has become a much less service-oriented business in recent years, so involved and caring sales-people are hard to find. Make sure you appear to be friendly with a ready smile and that you are well dressed.

ATTIRE
Wear:
- Conservative suit and tie
  or
- Tasteful blouse and skirt
- Socks
- Clean, shined shoes, without scuffs

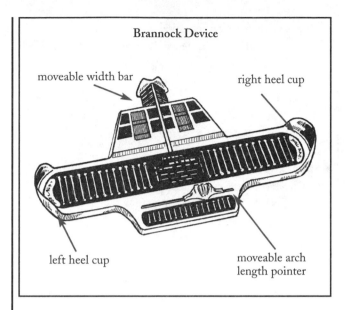

Brannock Device

moveable width bar

right heel cup

left heel cup

moveable arch
length pointer

Do Not Wear:
- Sneakers
- Flip-flops
- Heavy cologne or perfume

BUZZWORDS TO USE
- Brannock Device (the metal foot measurer)
- Slippage (either toe or heel)
- Trees (short for "shoe trees")

CRITICAL KNOWLEDGE
- A good fit should leave ¼-inch of room between the
  big toe and the tip of the shoe. There should be no
  slippage.

- Shoes with four or five eyelets will take a 36-inch lace, while athletic shoes will generally take a 40- to 45-inch lace.

Insider Tip
- If the patron needs a half-size larger but it is not available, substitute a "wide" style of the lower full size (i.e., a 7 wide for a 7½).
- Shoes that will be worn on a daily basis should be fitted at the end of the day, when the feet have expanded.
- "Toe length" refers to the total length of the foot.

HOW TO SURVIVE
AWKWARD ELEVATOR SILENCE

Mention current weather or temperature, time of day, day of week, month, season, or approaching holiday, and wait for comment. Other subjects of common experience include popular television programs, local sports teams, and the state of being tired. If silence continues, stare at elevator walls or floor until it reaches your destination. Exit immediately.

HOW TO DEAL WITH
A NIGHTMARE BOSS

The Control Freak

The Control Freak will attempt to micromanage your every task and responsibility.

✪ **Bombard him with information.**
Copy him on every e-mail even remotely involving him or his area of responsibility. Leave towering stacks of reports and copies of all correspondence on his desk. Include him in the most mundane meetings and discussions. You may be able to short-circuit his control mechanism with the sheer volume of data.

✪ **Solicit his opinion, but control the options.**
If you must leave a decision up to your boss, offer the solution you favor and two or three lame options—ridiculous or unworkable possibilities that will direct him to choose your course of action. Using phrases such as "You've probably already thought of this" and "I tried to put myself in your shoes when I worked on this" will help you gain favor.

✪ **Remain calm and pleasant.**
When your boss interferes with your work or second-guesses your decision, do not become defensive or combative. Say, "How ridiculous—I should have thought of that. Thank goodness I included you!" and

chapter 4: social disasters

then lead your boss back to your position, while encouraging him to think you're following his guidance.

★ **Continue to do your job.**
Bide your time. Your boss may ultimately believe that he's shown you the way and he can now go on to help others.

THE BUDDY

The Buddy will generally attempt to blur the lines between employee and supervisor, soliciting personal information and seeking inclusion as though you are the best of friends. Include the Buddy in small ways, but keep your distance.

★ **Invent a hobby.**
Avoid sharing intimate details of your real life by inventing a hobby, which you can discuss with her in minute detail. Your fictional toothpick sculptures or love of steam locomotives will become of great interest to the Buddy and can serve as the basis of your "friendship." Movies, restaurants, and sports are also safe, impersonal topics to raise.

★ **Offer social invitations you know she can't accept.**
Invite her to lunch on a day you are certain she has another appointment. Ask her out for a drink with "the gang" after work on the night she always goes to her yoga class, or when she will be away on business.

Be aware that she may proffer invitations in return, which easily can be evaded by inventing a nightly class of your own.

★ **Avoid hugs.**
If she attempts to throw a friendly arm around you, fake a sneeze. Blame allergies rather than perfume, which she can change. Your "allergies" can then also become a topic of friendly conversation.

THE WORKAHOLIC

The Workaholic has lost all sense of perspective, and has sacrificed his life to his job. He will expect the same of you.

★ **Present evidence of the real world.**
Replace all calendars he sees with ones depicting tropical retreats, ski slopes, or other vacation locales. Litter the office with travel brochures, and purchase office subscriptions to food, travel, and entertainment magazines. E-mail him regularly with weather updates of distant cities.

★ **Discuss family at every opportunity.**
Show him pictures of your family. Show him pictures of his own family. If even your most distant relative has bought a car, won a part in a school play, or suffered a toothache, offer these stories in careful detail—perhaps they will trigger recognition that he, too, has a wife, sister, uncle, or son.

★ **If he has ever discussed a personal interest, become obsessed with it.**
Pounce on any non-work-related subject in the hope of rekindling his own passion. Discuss popular subjects and pastimes to spark some vestigial interest. Try baseball, politics, food, music, and celebrity gossip. Avoid even juicy office gossip, since that will lead him back to work-related issues.

THE TELLER OF BAD JOKES

His jokes are always bad.

★ **Be prepared.**
Steel yourself for the punchline. If you are unable to determine if the punchline has been delivered, watch your boss for response cues such as a long pause or an expectant grin.

★ **Determine the nature of the required reaction.**
A secure boss will be satisfied with a friendly groan and head shaking, while an insecure boss will require a more elaborate show of amusement and appreciation. Respond accordingly.

★ **Fake amusement.**
THE SHOULDER SHAKE—Smile, cover your mouth with one hand, and shake your shoulders up and down. This is especially good for puns.
THE AMUSED CHUCKLE—Smile, look directly at your boss, and say, "Heh, heh, heh." This is a versatile, all-purpose laugh response.

The Genuine Guffaw—Smile broadly, then let out a single, loud "Ha!" Slap your thigh in amusement. If seated, slap your knee.

 Change the subject immediately.
Do not give him the chance to "tell you another one."

Be Aware

Be on guard for other styles of bad boss behavior, and prepare to take quick action:

• The Supreme Delegator

Always willing to accept all of the credit but none of the blame, the Supreme Delegator is really setting up others to take the fall. Although she tries to cloak her behavior in an air of confidence, the Supreme Delegator has very low self-esteem and fears that she will fail.

From the moment a project is handed off to you, through all the key decisions, to the final action, make sure you advise your boss—in writing—of all key decisions and plans. Keep copies. Do not be afraid to proceed as you think best, but be prepared for your boss to disavow all knowledge of the details should there be a problem.

• The Yes/No Manager

This boss is ever-increasingly bored with meaningful information, intelligent discussion, and any complexity. He wants every decision reduced to an overly simplified YES or NO.

Present an executive summary, with several alternatives for action. Attach the full report with well-reasoned, well-documented arguments for each point. If asked for your recommendation, give it orally.

- **THE PASSIVE-AGGRESSIVE BOSS**
The Passive-Aggressive Boss puts things off, then complains at the last minute that he has not had enough time. The boss can then blame those above or below him for doing a bad job.

   Be firm with deadlines and set them in writing. Involve others in the process when possible. These co-workers can then serve as witnesses to any mis-behavior on your boss's part.

- **THE INDECISION MAKER**
This boss ascended to power by a fluke—he can't actually make a decision himself. He needs input from three or four different sources in order to feel comfortable in his own shoes.

   Present any question to your boss as if you've taken an informal survey. Include information from any key employees he'd want to hear from.

- **THE ALL-BUSINESS-IS-PERSONAL MANAGER**
The All-Business-Is-Personal Manager has a seri-ously dysfunctional life outside of work, and thus cannot ever really separate business life from per-sonal life. He will take everything personally. He has nothing but work to cling to, so make your work time with him enjoyable. One bad day can ruin a whole relationship.

how to deal with a nightmare boss

HOW TO DEAL WITH A NIGHTMARE CO-WORKER

THE TALKER

The Talker just won't shut up.

⭐ **Look busy.**
Free time means chat time to the Talker. Leave paper-work handy on your desk, and spreadsheets or other documents open on your computer at all times. When the Talker approaches, stare at the task intently and pretend not to notice his arrival.

⭐ **Evade and deflect.**
Say, "I'd love to hear more, but I've got to finish this by [fifteen minutes from now]." Or, rise from your desk and say, "Oh my gosh, I've got to go to that meeting." As you walk away, suggest that another co-worker has expressed interest in whatever is on the Talker's mind and aim him in that direction.

⭐ **"Yes" the conversation to death.**
Talkers are often of the life-is-a-struggle type, for whom everything is a hardship, and they must con-vince you of this. As the Talker's tale unfolds, keep agreeing with the Talker, but be sure you do not ask a question or volunteer information. After five flat

agreements ("Yes . . . yes, I see.") the Talker should count this as adequate confirmation and wander off.

★ **Avoid showing emotion.**
Do not be cheerful around the Talker, as this may make her dejected and even more talkative. Do not be sad around the Talker, since this may encourage him to top your tale of woe with his own.

The Kiss-Up

The Kiss-Up craves approval mostly from the boss, but will also seek approval from you.

★ **Congratulate her on her dedication and achievements, no matter how dubious:**
"You've sure got a way with a spreadsheet," "It's not everyone who'd work five straight weekends," or "You make the *best* coffee."

★ **Get her to do some of your own work as well.**
Suggest that this is a good way to further bring her talents to the boss's attention.

★ **Avoid her during restructuring.**
During times of management turmoil or when the chain of command is uncertain, the Kiss-Up may become disoriented or hostile. Give her a wide berth.

The TMI (Too Much Information)

TMIs have no boundaries and no shame. Every unsettling piece of personal information is worth sharing with you.

★ **Avoid TMIs on Mondays.**
The weekend will provide him with an abundance of ammunition for inappropriate personal tales. By Tuesday or Wednesday, he may have expended the most harrowing of these stories on fellow workers.

★ **Do not get on an elevator with a TMI.**
If you see a TMI waiting for an elevator, take the stairs. If you are already inside the elevator, feign some activity—a forgotten wallet, pocketbook, or keys—that will provide an excuse for your quickly exiting to retrieve the item.

★ **Maintain a buffer of at least two co-workers between the TMI and yourself at any company party or off-site function.**
If the first co-worker bolts, you will still have time for evasive maneuvers as the TMI engages the second.

★ **Say, "Thanks for sharing."**
Upon the completion of a long and sordid tale—his tapeworm, his night on the town, or his dream about the boss—say "Thanks for sharing." Without further comment or response from you, the TMI will move on to seek a more appreciative audience.

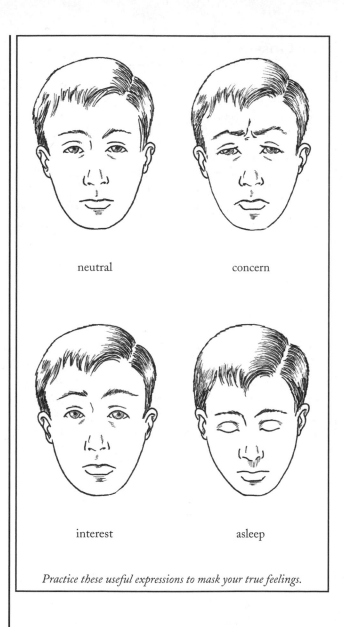

neutral

concern

interest

asleep

Practice these useful expressions to mask your true feelings.

The Gossip

While sharing many of the characteristics of the TMI, the Gossip specializes in spreading too much information about other people.

⭐ **Beware the signs.**
A sure sign of a hopeless (but amateur) gossip is someone who proceeds a statement with, "I shouldn't be telling you this but . . ." or, "I promised I wouldn't tell anyone but . . ." Apply the techniques for avoiding a TMI, on page 344, to save yourself from a gossip who wants to tell you everything.

⭐ **Bait and switch.**
Offer outrageous stories about yourself in order to stun and distract him from prying into your true private life. With a serious expression, tell the Gossip that you were locked in the monkey cage at the zoo all weekend and had the time of your life; or that you accidentally sent a very revealing personal photo via e-mail to all the executives in the company. The juicier the story, the better. When he asks, "Is that true?" say, "I'm sorry, I can't talk about it anymore."

HOW TO TEE OFF IN FRONT OF A CROWD

1 Relax.
Try to see the first tee as any other shot in the round. Do not make significant changes in your tempo. Try not to rush any aspect of your pre-shot routine or swing. Ignore comments from the crowd waiting to play, or pressure from the starter to speed up.

2 Warm up.
Thoroughly stretch in whatever way increases blood flow to your body and feels good. Take as many practice swings as you need.

Focus your thoughts on your mind, body, and swing.

how to tee off in front of a crowd

3 **Release the tension in your body.**
Identify where the tension is, consciously tighten that area of your body, and then consciously relax that area while noticing the difference. Take a deep breath—in through your nose and out through your mouth—before you hit.

4 **Be mindful.**
Tune in to your feelings prior to your first swing. Are you nervous? Anxious? Steeped in self-judgment? Be aware of these negative feelings and the consequences of them on your body. Recognize that these feelings often get in the way of your true golf swing and game. Replace those feelings with positive energy. Choose to feel competent and content. Remember a time when you played your best. Generate these thoughts until you are ready to hit the ball.

5 **Be confident about your abilities and expectations.**
If you hit the ball 200 yards 80 percent of the time, you will most likely hit the ball 200 yards this time. This does not mean that you should not strive for your personal best throughout the game. Recognize that the first tee is a starting point on which you are building a solid foundation for your day's golf game.

6 **Select the club with which you feel most comfortable.**
This may not be your driver. Use a long iron or three wood if your driver is not your best club off the tee.

7 | Follow a routine for addressing the ball.
Keep to an established pattern of how you walk up to the tee, how many practice swings you take, how you set your stance, and at what moment you start your swing. This routine is especially important on the first tee.

8 | Do not overanalyze your swing.
Your muscle memory will complete the swing for you if you cease to over-think it. Do not over-swing in an effort to hit the ball farther.

9 | Focus.
Choose a single location on the fairway and aim at that spot.

Be Aware

- Spend time on the practice tee prior to hitting off the first tee. Go through six to eight clubs in your bag—start with wedges (they are easy to swing) and work your way up to woods. Visualize hitting off the first tee on your last 10 to 12 practice drives.
- Golf is the culmination of physical, emotional, and mental preparedness. It is a game that begins and ends in both the body and the mind of the golfer. The first tee is the initial setting where you need to understand and accept the interrelation of these three elements.

HOW TO THWART
A GOLF CHEAT

Cheating at golf is so pervasive it seems to be part of the game: even people playing alone do it. There are mulligans off the tee, gimmies on the green, and lots of ways to get an unfair advantage in between. Here are a few of the most common scams and how to recognize and defeat them.

THE LOST BALL ROUTINE

While searching for a ball lost in the woods, the player drops another ball that he has been carrying and falsely announces to the group that he has found his original ball. He has saved himself a penalty stroke and has positioned the ball as he pleases. A variation on this play is to find a stray ball, claim it, hit it, and move on quickly.

Always keep an eye on your opponent.

1 | Make a mental note of the markings on your opponent's ball at the start of the round.
Notice color, scratches, brand, and number.

2 | Always help to look for a missing ball, and keep an eye on your opponent as well.
Two people searching also speeds up play.

IMPROVING A LIE

The cheat gently taps her ball with a foot or the club, gaining a more favorable position.

1 | Stand near your opponent so that you can see the ball at all times.

2 | Always watch your opponent, and, more important, let her know that she is being watched at all times.
Subtle comments about her technique, her attire, or the nuances of her address will let her know she's being carefully observed. You do not have to stand by her side all day long, but put yourself in a position where you can see any errant moves. Being under constant surveillance makes most people less inclined to bend the rules.

3 | Note how much of the ball is visible as you approach it, and mark its position in relation to nearby objects, such as roads, trees, and traps.
As the cheat goes to take the shot, the amount of the ball that is visible to you, even at a distance, should not change. Watch also for substantial changes in the ball's location; some players do not stop at simply tapping the ball to improve the lie.

Reporting Fewer Strokes

On a hole on which everything went wrong, she drops a few strokes from the score before announcing or recording it. She realizes that most opponents will lose track at around eight or nine strokes, and may not question such a total for fear of embarrassing themselves or the player.

1 Keep score carefully yourself.

2 Ask for a careful account of each stroke after every hole.
Be supportive of your golfing companion. When she has a difficult hole, tell her to hang in there, that it happens to the best, and so on—but when the hole is complete, ask her to recap the hole in a friendly, sympathetic manner.

Playing Dumb

Though he has hit his ball out of bounds, into the water, or in any other situation where penalty strokes are applicable, he tries to take only one penalty stroke where two are warranted.

1 At the completion of the hole, ask for a clear account of the score and applicable penalty strokes.

2 | If there is any debate, be courteous, but firm.
If the scoring remains unresolved, take it up with
the club pro at the end of the round.

Fake Handicap

Someone who has a five handicap introduces himself
to a group of strangers and announces a higher handicap. After shooting a 78, he claims that it was the
round of his life, and is somewhat sheepish about
taking everyone's money.

1 | Take out your own USGA handicap card as you are
having the discussion about handicaps.
Tell the stranger that you have all agreed to show each
other your cards before starting.

2 | At the end of nine holes, assess where this individ-
ual stands.
If it is clear that things are not what they appear,
demand an adjustment in his stated handicap. If he
balks, play the back nine, but state that the competition or bet is off. If someone you just met dumps
the front nine, scoring above his alleged handicap, be
cautious about increasing ("pressing") a bet on the
back nine. It could be a setup.

Be Aware

• Keeping an opponent honest requires you to be
observant and to hold everyone accountable for his
or her strokes as the round unfolds. This may seem

tedious at times, and may cause some odd inter-
actions with your opponents. You must decide
what is more important to you: interpersonal
relations or winning.

- Cheating can occur even when there is no betting
  or competition between players. A player seeking
  to claim a new course record or his own personal
  best score can seek to shave strokes from the score-
  card. You can decide how involved you want to be.

HOW TO DISARM
AN IRATE GOLFER

1 Determine the level of danger.
If a golfer is waving a club around angrily or drunk-
enly, or is exhibiting undue hostility, it may be necessary to act quickly to restore order and safety.

2 Try to talk him down.
Speak calmly, keeping your tone even and your voice
low. Do not make sudden gestures or movements.
Remind him that it's only a game. Tell him to take a
few deep breaths.

3 If he threathens to strike, quickly move into the
center of the potential swing.
As he draws the club back to swing at you, approach
him at an angle that will bring you to the center of
the club. Try to remain close to his body. You are
much more likely to be injured by the outer end of
the club.

4 Grab the club.
At the top of his swing, or just as the club starts
to descend, step close to him and, using one or both
hands, clutch the club tightly near the grip. Pull
down, staying close to him, until you can wrap your
arm around the club. Hold the shaft with your armpit
while keeping a firm grasp on the club's grip.

Grab here.

Grab the club of the irate golfer as it starts to descend or at the top of the swing.

Tuck the club under your armpit and wrench it away by rotating away from the irate golfer.

5 Wrench the club away.
Maintaining your hold, rotate your body around, away from the golfer's face. This maneuver should give you the leverage you need to wrench the club out of his grip. Pull with just enough force to free the club from his grasp.

6 Step back quickly, and be prepared for him to continue to be angry and to flail.
If necessary, use the club to keep him away from his bag, where he might obtain a second weapon.

7 If necessary, call for help.
Seek the assistance of your fellow golfers to help defuse the situation.

8 Continue to talk to him until he calms down.

Be Aware

It is always advisable to make all possible attempts to avoid physical confrontation. Your first choice should be to ignore and walk away from an irate golfer. Your next choice should be to use verbal skills to calm the golfer by speaking in low tones and showing understanding. Become physical only as a last resort, to avoid greater injury to yourself or others.

HOW TO CURE A
GOLF ADDICTION

1 Examine your behavior.

A golf addict is a person whose life is controlled by golf. You may think you have a problem with golf, but still not think that you are an addict. Ask yourself these questions. The total number of questions that you answer "yes" to is not as important as how you honestly feel about yourself as you answer these questions:

- Do you golf regularly? Do you feel empty inside if you cannot golf at your usual time?
- Do you ever golf alone, or watch golf alone?

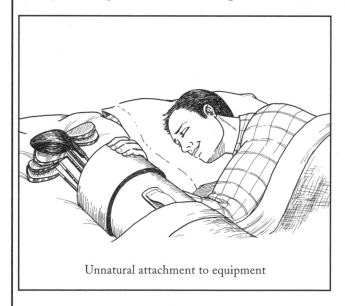

Unnatural attachment to equipment

- Have you ever substituted one club for another, thinking that one particular club was the problem?
- Have you ever cheated to obtain a better score?
- Have you ever lied to get into a golf course of which you were not a member?
- Has your job, family life, or school performance ever suffered from the effects of golf?
- Have you ever been arrested as a result of golf?
- Have you ever lied about the fact that you are playing, or about how much you play?
- Do you put the purchase of golf equipment ahead of your other financial responsibilities?

Watching golf alone

how to cure a golf addiction

- Have you ever suffered a golf-related injury?
- Do you continue to golf despite the fact that you are never satisfied with your performance?
- Does golf interfere with your sleeping or eating?
- Does the thought of not being able to play golf terrify you?
- Do you feel it is impossible for you to live without golf?

2 **Admit that you have a problem, and that you need help.**
You are not responsible for your disease—but you are responsible for your recovery. You can no longer blame people, places, and courses for your addiction.

Arrested due to golf activities

Playing alone

3   **Admit to one other person that you have a problem.** This person will help you wean yourself off the game. This person should not be a regular in your foursome.

4   **Reduce the amount of golf you play.** Going cold turkey may be difficult—first, reduce by half the number of times you play a week. Then cut that amount in half the following week, and so on. Replace golf with other activities to take your mind off the withdrawal you may experience. Make it a point to play other sports, go to the movies with your family, and watch alternate programming on Sunday afternoons.

5 Make direct amends to everyone you've harmed emotionally or physically as a result of your addiction.
This will help you to "own" your disease, and also allow others to help you when you need it.

6 Watch yourself carefully—and be willing to forgive a relapse.
Many addicts relapse at some point during recovery. If you fall back into your old ways, admit it to yourself first, then to others who can assist you in finding your way again.

7 Do not be afraid to ask for help when you need it.
Your golf pro may be able to direct you to others who have been through what you are dealing with. Form a support group. Therapists may also give you perspective. (Note: Sports therapy is physical therapy, not mental therapy.)

8 Remember that no one is perfect.
Seek the ability to change the things you can, and to accept the things you cannot change. Realize that you may never be able to play golf again without risk of a relapse. There is more to life than golf. But then again, relapses can always be cured.

How to Disguise a Beer Belly

short
sleeves

snug T-shirt

pants waist falls below gut

Wrong

structured
clothing

undershirt
(tucked in)

pants worn
to belly button

long sleeves
for proportion

Right

Draw attention away from gut.

HOW TO PUT OUT A GREASE FIRE

1 Do not douse with water.
Oil and water do not mix: Water will cause the burning oil to spatter and spread the fire. Do not move the burning pan to the sink.

2 Turn off the stove.

3 Put on an oven mitt.
Large mitts are the safest option. If barbecue mitts—those that cover the forearm—are available, use for added protection.

4 Find a lid that fits the pan.
A lid that is slightly larger than the pan will also work.

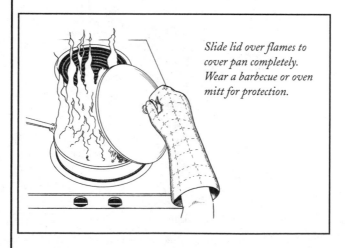

Slide lid over flames to cover pan completely. Wear a barbecue or oven mitt for protection.

5 | Hold the lid at an angle toward the fire.
Do not try to lower the lid directly onto the pan or you risk burning your arms. Keep your face and chest as far from the flames as possible.

6 | Slide the lid onto the pan and hold it in place until the pan cools.
The pressure from the heat and flame can force a lid off the pan. Hold it securely in place.

7 | Do not lift the lid.
Lifting the lid will add oxygen and feed the fire. Take the lid off only when the pan has become noticeably cooler.

8 | If no lid is available, use baking soda.
Dump a large amount of baking soda on the grease fire to extinguish it quickly. Avoid using baking powder, which can cause the fire to flare.

Be Aware

- Do not use a dry chemical extinguisher to try to put out a grease fire. It is not effective, and the force of the compressed chemical agent can splatter burning material and spread flames.
- Never leave cooking oil to heat unattended: Flames may develop quickly.

How to Treat a Grease Burn

1 | Cool the burned area.
Immediately run cold water over the burned area for several minutes or until the injury site is cool.

2 | Dry the burned area gently.
Blot the injury site using a clean, dry towel or sheet.

3 | Check for blistering.
If the blisters are small, pop them with a sterilized pin and remove dead skin using scissors. (Wiping the tip of a pin in alcohol or heating it in the flame from a match will adequately sterilize the pin.) If there are no blisters and the burn is less than one inch across, apply burn cream and a sterile dressing.

4 | Cover severe burns.
If the burn is larger than one inch across or is very blistered, cover it with a clean, dry sheet or towel and seek medical attention promptly.

Be Aware

- Infection is the main risk. Signs of infection include fever or local warmth, increased redness around the burned area, increased soreness, red streaks, swelling, or drainage of pus.
- Do not apply oily or greasy substances such as petroleum jelly or butter to the wound. These popular but misguided burn remedies are detrimental to the healing process.

HOW TO EXTINGUISH A CHRISTMAS TREE FIRE

1 Assess the size and nature of the fire.
Quickly determine if the source of the fire is electrical, and observe how large an area of the tree is burning. A fire larger than the size of a small wastebasket cannot usually be contained, even with a home extinguisher. If the fire is that large, evacuate the building and call the fire department from a cellular phone or a neighbor's house.

2 If the fire is small and not electrical, douse it or smother it.
Extinguish the fire with a bucket of water or a multipurpose (Class ABC) fire extinguisher, or smother it with a wet blanket.

3 If the fire is electrical, use a fire extinguisher.
Do not throw water on an electrical fire. Use a multipurpose (Class ABC) home fire extinguisher.

4 When using a fire extinguisher, stand with your back toward an exit, six to eight feet from the fire, and Pull, Aim, Squeeze, Sweep (PASS).
Pull the release tab, aim at the base of the fire, squeeze the lever to release the pressurized chemicals, and sweep from side to side as you slowly move closer to the fire.

If the fire is larger than the size of a small wastebasket or is spreading quickly, get out of the house.

5 | If the fire is still spreading, exit the house.
Evacuate the building quickly. Do not attempt to save
ornaments, Christmas presents, or other valuables.

How to Prevent a Christmas Tree Fire

1 | Select a fresh tree.
A dry tree is a major fire hazard; to get the freshest
tree, cut it yourself. If you purchase a precut tree, run
your hand down a branch to make sure it is not dry
and shedding needles. Test the tree by bending a needle:
If it snaps, the tree is too dry.

2 | Leave the tree in a bucket of water overnight.
Place the tree in the stand the next day. Water it daily.

3 | Place the tree at least three feet away from a fire-
place, radiator, or other heat source.

4 | Unplug tree lights when not in use.
Do not leave the lights on during the day, when you
go to bed, or when you leave the house.

5 | Do not place lit candles on or near a tree.
If tradition requires candles, use specially weighted
sconces that do not tip over. Do not add electric tree
lights or other electric equipment to or around the
tree (such as a train set), in the event that water
must be thrown onto the tree. Do not leave the tree
unattended.

HOW TO MAKE AN EMERGENCY MENORAH

If Hanukkah arrives and you are without a menorah or candles, you will have to make your own.

BAKED MENORAH

You will need 2 cups flour, 1 cup salt, 1 cup water, 9 nuts or washers (at least $1/2$ inch in diameter), a large mixing bowl, and at least three hours.

1 Preheat the oven to 200° F.

2 Mix the flour and salt together in the large bowl.

3 Add water.
Slowly pour water into the mixture and stir until it becomes the consistency of dough. If it is too dry, add more water; if it is too wet, add more flour.

4 Roll the dough into a strip about 12 inches long, 1 to 2 inches wide, and 2 inches thick.

chapter 4: social disasters

5 Cut a 1-inch piece off one end and press it into the center of the strip.
The center area will be raised slightly: It will hold the Shamos candle, which is used to light the other candles.

6 Add the nuts to the dough.
Press the nuts into the dough, four spaced evenly on each side of the Shamos holder. Place the ninth nut in the raised center portion. The nuts should be pushed in so that part of the nut sticks up above the top of the dough. The nuts are the candle holders.

7 Bake.
Place the menorah on a baking sheet, and place in the oven. Bake for about two hours. The menorah is ready when the dough becomes hard. (You can air dry the menorah instead of baking it; allow two to three days for hardening.)

8 Let cool.

Baked Menorah

Press nuts into the dough before baking.
Let menorah cool completely before use.

Bowl and Dirt Menorah

You will need a baking dish or bowl and sand, dirt, rice, or gravel.

 Fill a 2-inch-deep (or deeper) bowl with sand, dirt, rice, gravel, or other nonflammable material.
Stick the appropriate number of candles in the dish each night (placing the Shamos on a slightly elevated mound) to create a makeshift menorah.

Be Aware
Do not make a menorah out of wood. Hanukkah candles must be allowed to burn down completely, and wood presents the risk of fire.

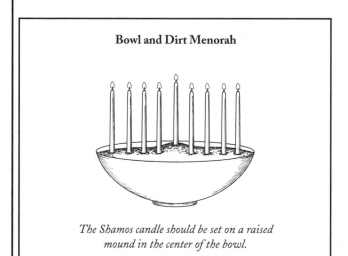

Bowl and Dirt Menorah

The Shamos candle should be set on a raised mound in the center of the bowl.

HOW TO DEAL WITH A BAD GIFT

★ **Do not lie.**
If you receive a gift you simply detest, do not compli-
cate the situation by lying. Do not praise the gift and
say that you've always wanted one: The giver may
later wonder why you are not using the gift or why
it is not displayed in your home—or you may get
something similar next year. If you receive an awful
sweater, say something neutral like, "I love sweaters."
If the giver is still not convinced that you like
the present, try it on; you may also be able to offer
another partially true compliment: "What a perfect
fit!" If you receive as a gift something you already
own, you do not need to advise the giver. Say, "I love
this [thing]. How did you know?"

★ **Thank the giver for the thought, not the gift.**
Say, "How thoughtful of you" or "Thanks for thinking
of me" or "I can't tell you how much this means to me."

★ **Do not overpraise the gift or the giver.**
Keep your thanks simple and brief.

★ **Determine where the gift was purchased.**
If there was no gift receipt, check the packaging,
label, and tags for a store name. If you cannot determine where it was purchased, ask the giver appre-
ciatively: "Where did you ever find this?" Note the
name in order to return the gift later.

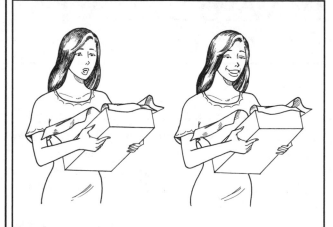

Do not show shock or disappointment when presented with a bad gift. Smile: Remember, it's the thought that counts.

 Regift it.
Unwrap the gift completely to make certain that it does not contain a hidden card, monogramming, or other giver- or recipient-specific identification. Rewrap it in fresh wrapping materials.

Be Aware
Regifting can be risky. You may later be embarrassed if you do not know where the gift you gave was purchased. Some regifts, particularly distinctive ones, may make the rounds (see "How to Repurpose a Fruitcake," facing page) and end up being regifted to the original giver, a situation you may find hard to explain.

HOW TO REPURPOSE A FRUITCAKE

★ **Turn the fruitcake into another dessert.**
Do not serve the fruitcake as is. Slice it very thin, tear the pieces apart, and use them in an English trifle, a dessert made with alternating layers of cake (née fruitcake), custard, whipped cream, and, sometimes, fresh fruit. Serve in a deep glass bowl (often called a trifle bowl).

★ **Use the fruitcake as a doorstop.**
Fruitcakes are very hardy and will last for years. Use the fruitcake to prop open a door.

★ **Use the fruitcake to prevent your car from rolling.**
When parked on a hill, wedge the fruitcake under the downhill side of a rear tire. In your garage, position the fruitcake on the floor as a tire stop to prevent the car from hitting the garage wall.

★ **Use the fruitcake as a dumbbell.**
A good-size fruitcake may weigh several pounds. Incorporate it into your exercise routine, holding it firmly for arm curls, or squeezing it between the feet for leg lifts.

★ **Use the fruitcake in a carnival game.**
Collect fruitcakes and stack them vertically in a pyramid. Using tennis balls, try to knock down the fruitcakes in five throws.

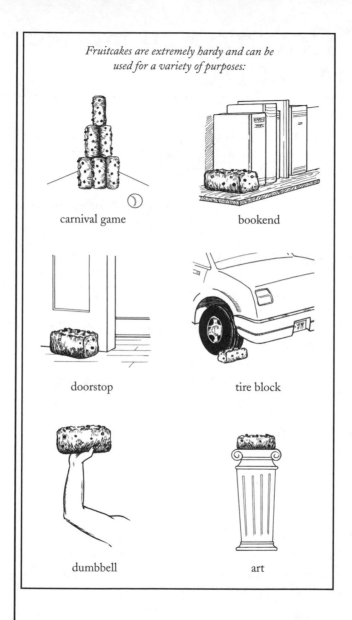

*Fruitcakes are extremely hardy and can be
used for a variety of purposes:*

carnival game

bookend

doorstop

tire block

dumbbell

art

★ **Use as bookends.**
Set up two fruitcakes either horizontally or vertically, depending on the size of the books.

★ **Use as art.**
Bolt a fruitcake to a painted board, frame it and hang it on your wall, or simply place it on a pedestal. Position the fruitcake in a well-lit area.

★ **Use the fruitcake as compost.**
Fruitcakes are made of (mostly) organic material, and make good fertilizer. However, it may take several years for the fruitcake to decompose.

How to Safely Eat a Fruitcake

1 **Slice it thin.**
Cut the fruitcake into narrow slices—no more than $3/8$ inch—while the cake is cool. Place the slices on a serving platter, cover, and allow to come to room temperature.

2 **Check the knife.**
After cutting, the blade should be somewhat sticky and slightly colored. If the knife does not have to be wiped with a damp cloth after each cut, the cake is too dry, and a healthy dollop of whipped cream will be necessary. If the knife is heavily streaked with cake ingredients after cutting, the fruitcake has not been baked long enough and may need to be repurposed.

3 Disguise the taste.
Cover with lots of ice cream and whipped cream. Wash the fruitcake down with strong black coffee, Irish coffee, brandy, or a hot toddy.

4 Swallow without chewing.
Cut the slice into small pieces. Swallow each piece whole, as you would a vitamin. If chewing is necessary, use your molars, not your front teeth or incisors, and try not to touch the food with your tongue, which has all your taste buds.

Be Aware

- Do not be fooled by a gift of a "Yule cake," "Christmas ring," or "dried fruit bread"—these are just other names for a fruitcake.
- If the fruitcake is very dark in color, it contains lots of molasses and corn syrup, making it exceedingly sticky, thick, and dense. The heavier the fruitcake, the more candied fruit and dark molasses it has. The darker or heavier the fruitcake, the more difficult it will be to swallow.
- A light-colored fruitcake is a good sign; the cake has plenty of batter and light corn syrup.
- Fruitcake should be stored in a cool place, such as a refrigerator or cellar. If kept cool and in a tin, the cake will last for at least a year, and you can give it as a present the following Christmas.

HOW TO FIT INTO CLOTHING THAT IS TOO TIGHT

For Men

1   **Wear newer shirts and pants.**
Garments (especially shirts) that have been laundered repeatedly are smaller than their original sizes. These items may also have loose buttons that might be ejected during a meal.

2   **Choose dark-colored garments.**
Lighter colors are less forgiving visually, while darker colors tend to obscure bulges.

3   **Move your collar button.**
Many men carry extra weight in the neck and jowls. Remove and reattach your collar button, moving it to the very edge of the collar tab. Wear a standard tie (not a bow tie) to hide the alteration.

4   **Wear suits.**
Suits are very effective for hiding pounds. They even out lines and offer structure to the body shape. Choose a dark-colored suit with a boxy shape rather than one cut narrow through the chest and waist. Shoulder padding is slimming, and is a must to balance the hips. (Broad shoulders help to create the

how to fit into clothing that is too tight

For Men

DO	DON'T

Move your collar button.

Wear fitted shirts.

Wear dark-colored, boxy suits.

Wear horizontal stripes.

Use the proper belt notch.

Wear single-vented suits.

ideal inverted triangle physique.) A suit jacket is also effective for hiding a large rear end: Choose a jacket with side vents/slits for extra room and comfort.

5 | **Move pants to below the belly.**
Do not attempt to hike pants up and wear them high on the waist: This will result in an unsightly bulge, the pants may not close properly, and they will be too short in length. Wear them low on the hips, and use a jacket or loose-fitting shirt to conceal the gut.

6 | **Use the proper belt notch.**
A belt should be worn in the third or fourth notch. Buy a longer belt rather than moving to a lower notch.

Be Aware

- Avoid fitted, knitted, polo-type tops, such as golf shirts. These garments accentuate what you want to hide.
- Avoid horizontal stripes, which widen your appearance.
- Avoid suits with a center vent in the back, which tends to ride on the rear end rather than fall over it.

For Women

1 Choose classic-fit trousers and tunic shirts and blouses.
Even if a bit tight, these garments will fit better and look more appropriate than severely cut items. Blouses can be worn untucked, but only if they are cut straight across the bottom and not high on the sides. If you carry extra weight in your hips, avoid narrow-leg pants; instead opt for classic or wide leg styles.

2 Use safety pins on pants with side and rear closures.
Safety pins can be used to extend the waistband and may even be used in a chain of two or three. Wear a long jacket or over-blouse to hide the pins; take care in windy conditions.

3 Pick structured garments.
Jackets and cardigan sweaters that have a structured shape—even without you in them—hide pounds. Look for jackets that have shoulder pads, back seams that curve, and tapered sleeves. Unlike the boxy suits men should wear, women's suits should be tapered, giving the appearance of a slimmer waistline.

4 Layer tops and use tops as shirt-jackets.
Blouses that are too tight when buttoned can be worn partially unbuttoned over a round-neck or turtleneck knit top. Leave the over-blouse unbuttoned down to a button above the waist; tuck the top and blouse into your skirt/pants for a slimming layered look. Add a jacket, or wear the blouse completely unbuttoned as a shirt-jacket if it is cut straight across the bottom.

For Women

DO	DON'T
 Wear tunic shirts and blouses.	 Wear spandex.
Use safety pins to close zippers.	 Wear flashy belts.
 Wear structured garments.	 Wear bulky sweaters.

how to fit into clothing that is too tight

5 Choose monochromatic ensembles.
Wear dark suits, or pair a black skirt or pants with a black top or blouse. To maximize the slimming effect of dark, monochromatic ensembles, keep the darkest garment on the bottom. Place lighter shades of the same hue near your face.

6 Wear bright colors properly.
To wear bright colors and still look thin, pair them with dark neutrals. Wear black pants/skirt with a brightly colored blouse or knit top, topped off with a black jacket. Or choose a red jacket with a black top and black pants/skirt.

7 Draw attention to the face with striking accessories, stylish hair, and tastefully applied makeup.

Be Aware
- Avoid clingy knits and spandex. These materials keep no secrets and tend to draw the eye to bulges. Lycra creates some stretch in a garment and is far more forgiving than spandex.
- Before the holidays, purchase a few blouses and two pairs of dark pants that are one size too big. Wear them before the holidays and people will think you've lost weight. After the holidays, they will fit perfectly.
- Avoid drawing attention to the waist with flashy belts over large shirts.

HOW TO SILENCE CHRISTMAS CAROLERS

★ **Turn out the lights.**
As soon as you hear or see the carolers coming down the street, douse the lights. A dark house may deter them from stopping, since they will think no one is home. Turning out the lights belatedly—after they have arrived at your door—will send a strong message, but carolers are frequently very determined.

★ **Turn up your music.**
Without opening your door, play CDs at high volume. Speed metal and 1970s rock are likely to be in a different key than the carolers, who will be unable to stay in tune, become discouraged, and depart. If you are listening to Christmas music, shut it off immediately, or they may be encouraged to sing along.

★ **Answer the door in a robe or towel.**
Embarrassed, the carolers may simply leave. Nudity (even partial) may offend them and make them unable to sing. Call to another person inside the house (real or imaginary), "I'll be right back."

★ **Answer the door holding a telephone.**
Shout, "I can't hear you! There are carolers singing!" into the mouthpiece until the carolers move on.

Answer the doorbell partially dressed
in order to frighten off carolers.

⭐ Bribe them.
Tell them you would like to make a small donation, and that you enjoy their singing—from a distance.

⭐ Request songs they will not know.
The song repertoire of the caroler is generally quite shallow. Good choices to stump the carolers include "Adam Lay Ybounden," "Riu, Chiu," and "The Zither Carol."

⭐ Send them to someone else.
Smile and point to the house of a stranger or a neighbor you dislike, and say, "My friend over there really loves carols!" A house that is lavishly decorated for the season will prove irresistible to them.

How to Sing Along When You Don't Know the Words

⭐ Request "Deck the Halls."
Every verse ends with "Fa La La La La, La La La La," which is easy to remember.

⭐ Just join in.
Carolers are irrepressible: If you are lost (or off-key), they will simply sing louder to drown you out.

⭐ Listen for the chorus.
Most carols have a repeating section, or chorus. Listen for it, and then sing only that part.

Lip-synch.
Move to the back of the group, then move your
mouth soundlessly as they sing.

Be Aware
- Do not attempt to discourage carolers by stating
  that you are Jewish: You will get "Light the
  Menorah," "The Dreidel Song," "Sunrise, Sunset,"
  or another menu of ethnic songs.
- Do not tell carolers that you don't celebrate
  Christmas: You are likely to hear "Frosty the
  Snowman," "Sleigh Ride," "Jingle Bell Rock,"
  or a litany of secular holiday songs.
- Do not attempt to avoid carolers by going to the
  bathroom; they will be waiting when you return.

HOW TO SURVIVE IF YOU HAVE NO ONE TO KISS ON NEW YEAR'S EVE

If You Are with Others

1 Keep a glass in your hand.
If others think you are being festive and uninhibited, you are much more likely to receive a kiss. Even if you are not drinking, always hold a partly full glass of champagne.

2 Hug people.
As the clock strikes midnight, begin hugging everyone around you.

3 Select a desirable person.
As you are hugging, look for an attractive person who you would enjoy kissing and who might kiss you. If a person is not randomly kissing others, he or she may be less likely to kiss you.

4 Begin your approach.
Act casual, but keep your destination in view. Slowly move toward your chosen one, hugging everyone on the way.

5 | Time your arrival.
Do not appear to be "lining up" to kiss this person. Time your arrival precisely as the person releases the previous reveler.

6 | Yell first, then hug.
Yell "Happy New Year!" as you move in. Hug, embrace, then pull away slightly.

7 | Kiss.
Keep your mouth closed, pucker slightly, and plant the kiss.

IF YOU ARE ALONE

★ Kiss a pet.
Dogs are generally agreeable and have relatively clean mouths. Cats are usually well groomed but are more passive and tend to get rather than give. Keep your mouth closed.

★ Kiss yourself.
Find a mirror, pucker up, lean close, and kiss. Keep the lips slightly parted. Do not attempt to use your tongue. Wipe the mirror clean after you have completed your kiss. You may also try kissing the back of your hand.

★ Kiss a celebrity.
Watch a favorite movie or show on television and kiss the screen when an appealing star has a close-up.

*If no humans are available to kiss at midnight, try kissing a pet.
Keep your mouth closed.*

Wipe the screen first to remove static electricity and dust, and wipe the screen after to remove any evidence.

★ **Hug a pillow.**
Full-body pillows are more satisfying.

★ **Call a friend on the phone.**
After you wish your friend a happy New Year, give the telephone mouthpiece loud, smacking kisses. (This works less well with cellular phones.)

CHAPTER 5

DOMESTIC DANGERS

HOW TO DEAL WITH WEDDING-NIGHT JITTERS

1 Eat.
You've probably been so busy and excited that you didn't have a chance to eat at the reception. Have some food now.

2 Postpone physical contact.
Unwind from the stress and excitement of the wedding before heading to the bedroom. Do something you both enjoy: Get an ice cream, take a stroll in a park, or just sit in a quiet place and talk about the day.

3 Eat mood-enhancing food.
Chocolate is an excellent mood enhancer: It contains the stimulants caffeine, theobromine, and phenylethylamine, as well as anandamide, a chemical—also produced naturally by the brain—that may enhance feelings of well-being.

4 Get the room ready.
Dim the lights, adjust the temperature, light scented candles, and put on soft music. Keep juices, bottled water, and fresh fruit on hand to rehydrate, rejuvenate, and reinvigorate.

5 Get yourselves set.
The bride and groom should be relaxed, comfortable, and confident. Offer a foot rub. Use lavender soap and scent to promote relaxation. Put on a cozy nightgown or robe over sexy lingerie or underwear.

6 Do something you've never done before.

How to Revive Your New Spouse

⭐ Brew coffee.
Pass a mug of coffee repeatedly under your spouse's nose.

⭐ Begin undressing your spouse.
Remove his socks to cool his body, then follow with his shirt, pants, and underwear. Most people will wake up if they sense they are being undressed.

⭐ Rub ice cubes over your spouse's body.
Start with the forehead, wrists, and soles of the feet. Keep going.

⭐ Apply pressure to the nail bed.
Take the tip of one of your spouse's fingers and hold it between your thumb and index finger. Very gently, apply steady pressure to the nail bed. Do not squeeze too hard. This method, used by emergency personnel to determine unconsciousness/unresponsiveness in victims, causes sharp pain. It should revive your partner quickly.

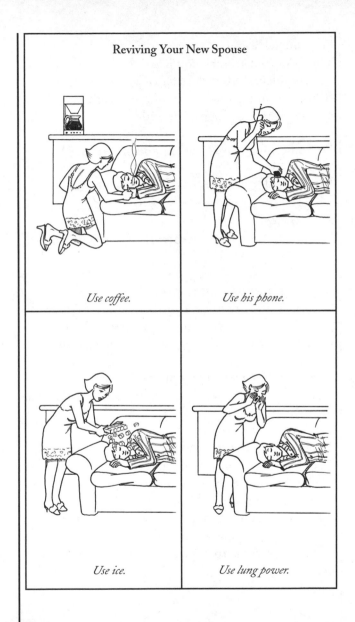

★ Tickle.

★ Call on the telephone.
If you are in a hotel, call the front desk and ask them to ring your room. Or call your spouse's mobile phone from your mobile. Most people will respond to the sound of a ringing phone.

★ Pretend there is an emergency.
Yell "Fire!" "Earthquake!" "Muggers!" and "Watch out!" repeatedly to get your spouse's adrenaline flowing. Once your spouse is awake, you can explain that you weren't ready for your special night together to end.

HOW TO SURVIVE
A HONEYMOON
DISASTER

Extreme Sunburn

1 Expose damaged skin to air.
Remove all clothing around the burn area: Clothing will irritate the burn site and may cause increased pain.

2 Drink water.
Drink at least 32 ounces of water to help promote sweating, which cools the skin.

3 Apply a cold compress.
Put ice in a plastic bag, wrap in a cotton T-shirt or other fabric, and apply to the burn area. If the burn area is very large, soak a bed sheet in ice water and apply it instead of a compress. Let the skin cool under the compress for 15 minutes to help reduce pain.

4 Apply a soothing gel or ointment to the burn area.
Carefully rub a cooling aloe lotion into the burned area. This is especially soothing if the aloe has been chilled in a refrigerator or a bucket of ice. Do not apply suntan lotion, baby oil, petroleum jelly, or any other foreign substance to the burn.

5 | Take pain medication.
Ibuprofen will help reduce pain at the burn site.

6 | Lie still.
Lie in a position that best exposes your sunburn to the air without coming into contact with the bed, your clothing, or another person. Do not bend sunburned joints.

7 | Continue with your honeymoon.
Take advantage of loose-fitting island fashions as your sunburn heals.

Be Aware
Depending on the severity of the sunburn, a new layer of skin will replace the burned area in two days to two weeks.

MIGRAINE HEADACHE

1 | Dim the lights.
Bright lights may exacerbate a migraine or prolong symptoms. Keep the shades drawn and the room lights off or very low.

2 | Reduce noise levels.
Turn off the radio and television. The room should be silent, or with soothing "white" noise such as that created by a small fan.

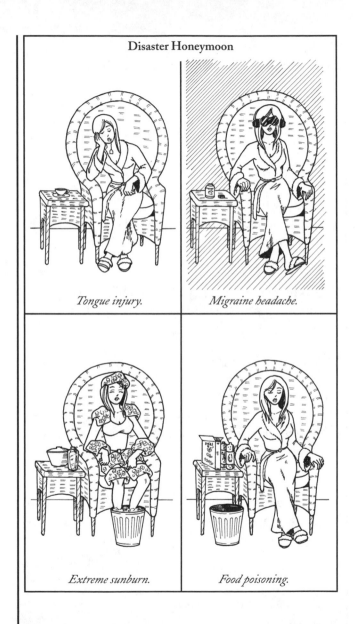

Disaster Honeymoon

Tongue injury.

Migraine headache.

Extreme sunburn.

Food poisoning.

3 | Limit movement.
Running, walking, and even climbing stairs may increase the intensity of a migraine.

4 | Eat vitamin-rich foods.
Magnesium and vitamin B2 (riboflavin) may combat migraine symptoms. Spinach, Swiss chard, and many nuts are high in magnesium, while mackerel, shad, and other oily fish are rich in riboflavin.

Be Aware
A migraine may last as little as one hour or as long as three days.

ACUTE TONGUE INJURY

1 | Prepare a tea bag.
Soak a tea bag in warm water for 2 minutes. Let it stand 1 minute at room temperature, then wrap it in gauze or a clean cloth napkin.

2 | Apply tea bag to tongue.
Place the moist tea bag on the injury site and press steadily. The tannic acid in the tea is a natural coagulant and should stop the bleeding. The tongue has a large number of blood vessels near the surface and will bleed profusely until the blood coagulates.

3 | Rinse.
Swish and spit using an anesthetic mouthwash, if available.

4 | Apply a numbing agent.
Apply ice to the wound to numb and reduce pain.

5 | Avoid acidic and salty foods and liquids.
Acidic substances, such as citrus fruits and vinegar,
and those high in salt, such as nuts and potato chips,
may aggravate the injury.

6 | Keep the tongue still.
The tongue will heal more quickly if it is inactive.

7 | Protect the tongue.
Wear an athletic mouth guard to protect the tongue
until the injury heals.

FOOD POISONING

1 | Stay hydrated.
Drink several gallons of water a day.

2 | Replenish mineral salts.
Nibble on dry salted crackers or plain rice to replace
salt lost through diarrhea.

3 | Do not induce vomiting.
Vomiting will not remove the bacterial culprit, but
will cause dehydration.

Be Aware

- Do not drink the water when traveling to the tropics or when you are unsure of its cleanliness. Avoid ice cubes in drinks, brushing your teeth with tap water, opening your mouth in the shower, or swallowing—or even rinsing your mouth with—water in swimming pools or the ocean.
- Only eat fruit that you can peel yourself. Avoid all vegetables and fruits that could have been washed in contaminated water, or fruits (like melons) that might have been soaked in water to increase their size and weight.
- If you don't know what it is, don't eat it.

HOW TO SURVIVE IF YOU FORGET YOUR ANNIVERSARY

⭐ Order an emergency bouquet.
Many florists can assemble arrangements with little notice. If you have just minutes to prepare, scour your neighborhood flowerbeds for daisies. Wrap them in colorful ribbon and present them as your initial gift.

⭐ Buy chocolates.
Most supermarkets and drugstores carry chocolate assortments. Choose a tasteful boxed set rather than several loose candy bars tied with ribbon.

⭐ Create a voucher card.
Prepare a card or piece of paper that shows the wonderful gift you're giving but can't give now because it isn't ready yet. Draw a picture of the gift on the card or paper.

⭐ Apologize, apologize, apologize.
If you're caught with nothing, making excuses will not help your case. Your level of contrition should be so extreme that your spouse begins to feel bad because you feel so terrible.

⭐ **Give an intangible present.**
Give her a homemade certificate for a weekend spa getaway. It could be for her only, or for a romantic weekend for both of you—a "second honeymoon" (but don't push your luck). A week free of household chores, a weekend of breakfasts in bed, or getting her car detailed are other possibilities.

How to Sleep on the Couch

1 **Remove the back cushions.**
If the couch has loose back cushions, take them off to add more width to the sleeping surface.

2 **Remove the arm cushions.**
Side cushions take up precious head and leg room, and will just end up on the floor in the middle of the night anyway.

3 **Fluff and flip.**
If the sofa design permits, remove the seat cushions, fluff them, then flip them so the side that was down is now the top. This will provide a more even sleeping surface.

4 **Cover the seat cushions with a sheet.**
The sheet will protect your face from odors trapped in the cushions and will protect the seating area from saliva.

First Anniversary

Tenth Anniversary

5 | Use your usual pillow.
You will sleep better with your head resting on a familiar pillow. Get yours from the bedroom, if the bedroom is still accessible to you.

6 | Depending on the temperature of the room and your comfort level, get a sheet, blanket, comforter, or large towel to put on top of you.

7 | Relax.
Do not to go to bed angry.

Be Aware
If you are an active sleeper, lay the sofa cushions next to the sofa to break your fall should you roll off during the night.

HOW TO GET YOUR BABY TO SLEEP

⭐ **Swaddle the baby.**
Fold down one corner of a receiving blanket and place the baby on top of the blanket with his head above the fold. Pull one side of the blanket securely across the baby's chest and tuck it underneath his body. Then pull up the bottom, folding the edge back, and finish by pulling the remaining side of the blanket across the baby's chest and underneath the body. The baby should fit snugly inside the blanket.

⭐ **Sway.**
Hold the swaddled baby close to your chest. Shift your weight from one foot to the other. This rhythmic stimulation will induce a sleepy state in the baby. Position the child so that his ear is over your heart. The beating will soothe him.

⭐ **Generate soothing white noise near the baby.**
Sound produced by a clothes dryer, dishwasher, blender, coffee grinder, hair dryer, vacuum cleaner, lawn mower, leaf blower, or air conditioner has a lulling potency that many babies cannot resist. Metronomes and ticking clocks can also soothe a baby to sleep by reminding a child of his mother's heart beat.

★ **Put the baby on a washing machine or dryer.**
Turn on the machine and set to normal cycle. The vibrations and noise are sleep-inducing. Do not leave the baby unattended.

★ **Go for a drive.**
The steady vibration of the car will have most infants asleep quickly. Open the window a crack and the air will keep you awake while the sound of the wind functions as soothing white noise for the baby. Do not get behind the wheel if you are exhausted and cannot operate heavy machinery.

Vibrations from a washer or dryer are sleep-inducing.

★ **Dance to music with a strong beat.**
Hold the child securely in your arms and bounce, twirl, and dip in a rhythmic fashion. Concentrate on moving the baby to the beat. The nonstop, steady jiggling will overload the brain's processing center. Avoid atonal, early-twentieth-century classical music, bebop, or any other music that could be jarring. Better choices include reggae, house, dance/trance, disco, minimalist, and pop.

★ **Climb up and down a staircase.**
Make sure your grip is tight around the baby. Go up and down at a rapid, steady pace.

★ **Use a pacifier.**
A pacifier (also known as a binky, paci, dummy, comforter, fooler, ninny, soother, soothie, or yum yum) can be an extraordinarily potent sleep inducer for some babies, but it can be habit-forming, and may cause problems if lost or stolen.

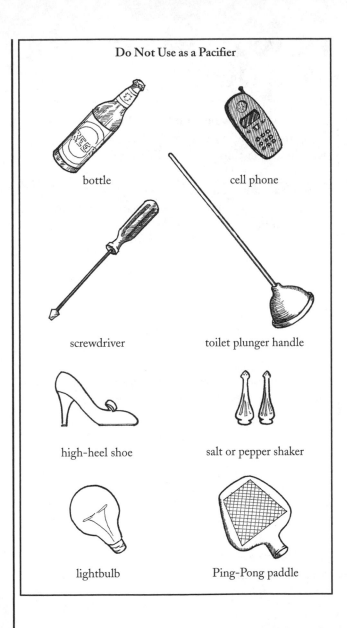

Do Not Use as a Pacifier

bottle

cell phone

screwdriver

toilet plunger handle

high-heel shoe

salt or pepper shaker

lightbulb

Ping-Pong paddle

HOW TO BABYPROOF THE HOUSE

1 Crawl around on your hands and knees to see the house from your child's point of view.
Anticipate the things that will interest him.

2 Remove all sharp edges.
Create corner bumpers out of foam or bubble wrap. Protect all hard edges within the child's reach, including coffee tables, end tables, bookcases, televisions, entertainment centers, hard chairs, dressers, bed stands, and desks.

3 Protect electrical outlets.
Use spring-loaded release covers in electrical outlets; plastic slip-in outlet guards can be too easily removed. Alternatively, move electrical outlets higher on the wall, to just below the ceiling, or replace all electrical appliances with battery-operated appliances. Batteries are toxic, however.

4 Install window guards.
Use window guards that prevent windows from opening more than 4 inches. Use the sliding button guard or the lock-and-key guard (which also keeps burglars out, but might prohibit a fast exit in an emergency). Protect low-to-the-ground windows with a hard plastic sheet or soft Mylar coating that prevents a child from shattering the glass. Do not use tilt-out windows

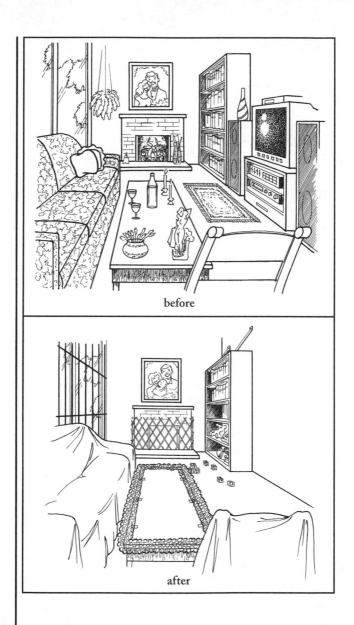

before

after

413. *how to babyproof the house*

unless windows are kept closed and locked at all times. Alternatively, install bars not more than 2⅜ inches apart on the outside of windows.

5 | **Install childproof doorknob spinners.**
Deter your child from entering unsafe rooms or closets by covering all doorknobs with childproof covers that will spin loosely when a child attempts to turn the knob.

6 | **Install drawer and cabinet guards.**
To prevent your child from reaching knives in a drawer or cleaning agents under the sink, secure drawers and cabinets with childproof latches.

7 | **Hang towels over the top of doors to prevent the child from slamming the door on his fingers.**
Alternatively, remove all doors.

8 | **Bolt heavy furniture to walls.**
Tall, heavy furniture can be tipped and pulled down by children, especially if they are climbing. Strap or secure bookcases, dressers, cabinets, and televisions. Tape lamps to tables or floors.

9 | **Avoid entanglements.**
Tie up (or down) or remove all curtains, blinds, and cords, especially electrical cords.

10 | **Remove poisonous plants.**
If you are not sure which plants are poisonous, throw them all away. Eliminate hazardous outdoor plants as well as houseplants.

11 Install baby gates.
Use gates that are 30 inches tall and have only vertical posts, with a bar top and bottom: Do not use diamond-shaped accordion gates that a child can climb. Place a gate at the top and bottom of a staircase. Keep gates closed at all times, even when the baby is asleep or not home.

12 Block the fireplace.
Put a nontoxic plant or fake logs in the grate. Install a gate around the outside of the hearth to prevent the child from approaching the fireplace or from sustaining an injury after hitting the edge of the fireplace. Put away all fireplace tools. Do not use the fireplace for actual fires until the child is older.

13 Reduce the temperature of the hot water heater.
Turn the water heater to 120°F or below to prevent scalding.

14 Install a spout guard over the bathtub spigot.
Mount foam on the metal faucet to prevent inadvertent head gouging or bumping while bathing.

15 Install a stove guard.
Attach a plastic shield in front of your stove's burners to prevent your child from reaching up and overturning pots and pans or burning fingers on hot or flaming surfaces. Affix knob protectors so your child cannot accidentally turn on the range.

Do not allow the baby to watch a dog drinking from the toilet.

16 Put lid guards on all toilets.
Do not let the baby watch a dog drink from the toilet bowl.

17 Line floors with gym mats.
Cover all flat surfaces with gym mats several inches thick to provide extra padding in case of a fall.

Be Aware
Keep purses and diaper bags, which are repositories for dangerous items and choking hazards, out of the reach of children. Put away guests' bags as well.

HOW TO SURVIVE BABY-GEAR OVERLOAD

1 Wear cargo pants.
Fill the pockets with soft items:
- Burp cloth
- Bibs
- Change of clothes (for you and for baby)

2 Dress the baby in cargo pants.
Fill the pockets with small necessities:
- Baby's cap
- Small board book for entertainment
- Teething ring

3 Wear a photographer's or fisherman's vest.
Fill the pockets with necessities:
- Small camera and film
- Baby blanket
- Crib toy
- Baby manual
- Hand sanitizer
- Bowl and spoon
- Changing pad
- Shampoo
- Nail clippers
- Bath soap
- Fever-reducing medicine

how to survive baby-gear overload

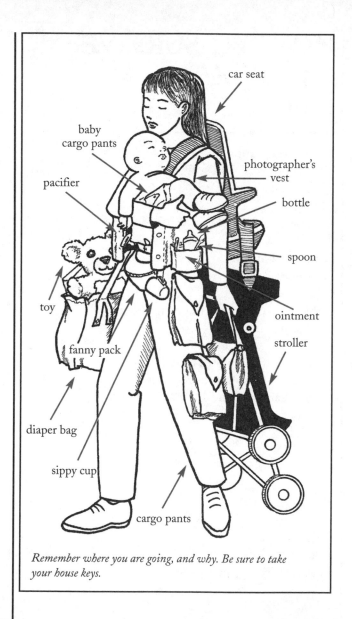

car seat

baby
cargo pants

pacifier

photographer's
vest

bottle

spoon

toy

ointment

fanny pack

stroller

diaper bag

sippy cup

cargo pants

*Remember where you are going, and why. Be sure to take
your house keys.*

- Teething gel
- Anti-itch cream
- Saline drops
- Nasal bulb syringe
- Thermometer
- Tissues
- Meat tenderizer for bee stings
- Adhesive bandages
- Antibiotic ointment
- Toothbrush and paste
- Plastic bag for soiled diapers
- Plastic bag for wet/dirty clothes

4 Wear a fanny pack.
Fill with adult necessities:
- Keys
- Wallet
- Headache medicine
- Sunglasses
- Makeup
- Cell phone
- Shopping list
- Pen

5 Circle your waist with a web belt.
Attach a canteen (for you) and a bottle or sippy cup (for baby).

6 Clip a pacifier to the baby.

7 | Sling a messenger bag across your back.
Fill with remaining necessities:
- Umbrella
- Toys
- Diapers
- Diaper wipes
- Cotton balls
- Sunscreen
- Diaper cream
- Juice
- Crackers
- Video camera

8 | Wear a baby carrier or sling.
Place the baby in the carrier and go. Remember where you are going, and why, and be sure to take your house keys with you.

HOW TO BREAK INTO YOUR CAR IF YOUR BABY IS LOCKED INSIDE

1 Maintain visual contact with your baby.
Observe her medical condition. Trick your baby into thinking that you meant to create this situation. See "How to Keep Your Baby Calm" on the following page.

2 Try a key from a similar model of car.
Ask passersby if they drive the same type of car. Ask if they will try to open your door with their key.

3 Use a coat hanger to break in.
Bend a wire hanger into a long J. Square off the bottom of the J so that the square is about two inches wide. Slide the hanger into the door, between the window and the weather stripping. Feel for the end of the button rod and, when you have it, pull it up to open the lock.

4 Break the window.
Don a pair of gloves, mittens, or socks to protect your hands from abrasion and injury. Select the window farthest from your child—a front window is ideal. Use a sharp object to punch through the middle of the window—try a rock, hammer, crowbar, piece of concrete from a broken curb, or even a concrete parking spot

how to break into your car if your baby is locked inside

marker. Hit the window with enough force to break the surface tension on the glass. Do not use your fist or a blunt object, neither of which will break the glass.

5 | Call for help.
Police officers and firefighters sometimes carry keys or lock-pick tools, or call a locksmith. A professional can often spring the lock in as little as three seconds with no damage to your car.

Be Aware
- In cold weather, do not warm up the car with the child inside. Many new cars automatically lock the doors once the ignition is turned on.
- Larger glass panels are less expensive to replace than fixed panels, such as small quarter panels.

How to Keep Your Baby Calm

★ | Pretend to be calm yourself.
The baby will feed off of your fear if you reveal it.

★ | Play peek-a-boo.
Begin with the standard hands-in-front-of-face style, then try hiding your face with a scarf or hat, and finally pop up from below various windows.

★ | Enlist the help of passersby.
Select friendly-looking people and people with babies who can coo at your baby through the window. Keep your child entertained and happy.

✪ Hoist a small dog in front of a window.
Turn the dog around to show its funny wagging tail.

✪ Hold up a magazine.
Turn the pages in front of the window so baby can see bright images.

✪ Use makeup to color yourself like a clown.
Smear lipstick on lips (go beyond true lip outline), cheeks, and tip of nose. Use eyeliner and eyeshadow to accentuate happy eyes and eyebrows.

✪ Do vigorous calisthenics.
Babies think it's funny to see big people jump around.

Enlist the help of passersby to keep your child entertained.

how to break into your car if your baby is locked inside

HOW TO MAKE YOUR CHILD EAT VEGETABLES

⭐ **Eat vegetables yourself.**
Be enthusiastic about vegetables. "Beans are awesome!" "Peas rule!" "Rutabagas rock!"

⭐ **Talk in euphemisms.**
Encourage your child by calling the vegetable a "growing food" or "brain food" or "run-fast food" or "beauty food."

⭐ **Require one bite.**
Even if she does not like it, with the "one-bite rule" the child should eventually grow accustomed to the taste, though it may take years.

⭐ **Let the child select the vegetable.**
Take your child to the grocery store to pick out one vegetable. Invite her into the kitchen to help you prepare it for dinner. She will become emotionally invested in the vegetable and proud of it. She may not only eat the vegetable, she may urge others to do so.

⭐ **Sneak vegetables into other dishes.**
Camouflage vegetables in stews, lasagna, pot pies, pizza toppings, casseroles, or soups.

Arrange vegetables in unusual ways.

★ Change presentation.
Arrange vegetables in a happy face. Use unnaturally colored ketchup (pink, green, blue) to jazz up a pile of vegetables. Make trees with broccoli and asparagus, boats from endive, and a lake out of guacamole.

★ Prepare the vegetable in different ways.
If she rejected the steamed broccoli, next time serve it raw with a dip. If the asparagus in cream sauce was not popular, try it with butter and lemon. Use a blender or a juicer to transform the vegetable into a purée or a smoothie.

★ **Make vegetables the only option.**
Designate "vegetarian night" and serve nothing but vegetables. Your child will eat them if she is hungry and there is no other food available. When the meal is over, declare the kitchen closed and do not allow snacks or dessert.

★ **Do not make food into a battle of wills.**
Be matter-of-fact about whether your child does or does not eat her vegetables. Do not force a vegetable on your child or bribe her to eat. Do not say, "If you eat your brussels sprouts, you can have dessert." This will interfere with her developing a genuine affection for the vegetable, and reinforce sweets as the truly desirable food.

HOW TO TRACK YOUR TEENAGER'S MOVEMENTS

How to Determine If Your Child Is Driving Your Car

1 Purchase an inexpensive, analog watch.

2 Place the watch behind a rear tire of your car.
Place the watch before you go to bed at night or away on a trip. If your car is not parked so that it has to be backed up to be moved, place another watch in front of a front tire.

3 Check the watch.
In the morning or on your return, examine the watch. If your child has taken the car while you were away, it will have been crushed, stopping the machinery at the exact time and date.

Place watch under tire.

How to Determine If Your Child Is Sneaking Out at Night

1 After your child goes to his room for bed, remove a hair from your head.

2 Attach the hair to the door of your child's room. Use saliva to place one end of the hair on the doorframe and the other on the door itself.

3 Wake up earlier than your child in the morning.

4 Check for the hair.
If your child has left the room during the night, the hair will have become detached or fallen off.

Be Aware

• If your teenager's room has a window to the garden, water the garden thoroughly each night and rake the dirt smooth. Look for footprints in the morning.

• If you do not have enough hair for the door-hair alarm, if your teen needs to open the door to go to the bathroom, or if a pet might dislodge the hair, grease the front door knob with butter. Check in the morning to see if the knob has been wiped clean so it could be turned and the door opened.

HOW TO SURVIVE EMPTY-NEST SYNDROME

1 Allow yourself time to grieve.
Sadness is a natural reaction to your child's departure.
Permit yourself to cry now and again without shame.

2 Find a temporary replacement for your affection.
To ease the transition, get a pet, or take your child's
photo to a copy center and get a life-sized replica.

3 Wean yourself.
- Rearrange furniture in your entire house, not just in
  your child's room. A new look can make you feel
  like you have entered a new stage of life.
- Remove the most recent photos of your child. Recent
  photos can be a reminder that he was recently in the
  house—replace them with older images.
- Establish a "Reminder Jar." Similar to a "Swearing
  Jar" into which a parent places money for every
  swearing infraction, this jar reinforces behavior modi-
  fication and punishes "remember when" infractions.

4 Convert your child's room into your own space.
Install a Murphy or sofa bed so that your child will have
a place to stay when he comes home for visits, but alter
the primary function of the room permanently. Set up a
home theater, exercise room, or greenhouse.

Return to your pre-child life.

5 Return to your pre-child life.
- Read a book.
- Invite your friends over for dinner.
- Fire the maid.
- Enjoy the quiet and calm.
- Watch the television shows you want to watch.
- Find things just where you left them.
- Take a trip.

Be Aware

Keep a list of the things your child did that annoyed, frustrated, and angered you. When you start to recall these things with fondness and a smile, you will have successfully entered the next phase of your life.

HOW TO SURVIVE
IF YOUR CHILD
MOVES BACK IN

⭐ Be sensitive to your child's needs—for a while.
Sometimes a child returns home because of a negative life change. Be understanding, and realize that a child moving back home is a difficult situation for all involved. Do not let yourself be exploited, however.

⭐ Charge rent.
Match market rates—deep discounting will only encourage your child to stay where it's cheap and easy.

⭐ Assign chores.
More people means more work, so delegate laundry folding, mowing the lawn, cleaning the porches, washing dishes, raking leaves, and other tasks. Do not offer to pay an allowance. If other family members have also moved in—your son- or daughter-in-law or grandchildren—give them chores as well.

⭐ Motivate change.
Place the classified advertisements section of the newspaper by your child's door. Do not change the message on your answering machine. Do not provide him with meals, change his bed linens, or allow him to watch television in the family room.

★ Do not alter your new lifestyle.
Continue to host your book group, bridge club, and cocktail parties. Continue to use his old room for its new purpose—sewing, exercising, big screen television watching.

How to Prevent Reentry

★ Change the locks.
Change the alarm code, too.

★ Paint the house.
He might not recognize an unfamiliar color.

★ Hide the car.
Park around the corner.

★ Put a different name on the door/mailbox.

★ Get a large, unfriendly pet.
Any size dog or cat can be effective if he is allergic.

★ Move to a smaller place.

★ Disappear.
Go on an extended vacation, rent an RV, or simply move out of town. Turn off your cell phone. Do not leave a forwarding address.

Put a different name on the mailbox.

Get a large, unfriendly pet.

new lock

Change the locks.

Disappear.

Be Aware
Parenting is forever.

CHAPTER 6
OUT AND ABOUT

HOW TO STEER YOUR BIKE DOWN A ROCK FACE

A wrong turn can send your mountain bike down a sheer rock face.

1 **Choose a line to follow.**
The instant you feel the bike pitching forward down-slope, look ahead of you and choose the line that you will follow down the rock face. The line should be as free of large boulders, drop-offs, and deep ruts as possible. Follow this line.

2 **Adjust your seating position.**
Move slightly "out-of-saddle," above the seat with your knees bent, similar to a jockey on a horse running down the stretch. Keep your weight shifted toward the back of the saddle, or behind it, to counteract the pull of gravity.

3 **Move the pedals to the 3 and 9 o'clock positions.**
Keep your feet on the pedals, with the pedals positioned across from one another. Do not put your feet straight up (12 o'clock) and down (6 o'clock), where the risk of making contact with rocks or the ground is greater. It is also more difficult to maintain a level position with the pedals straight up and down.

elbows bent

"out-of-saddle" position

knees bent

pedals at 3 and 9

Choose a line to follow down the rock face.

4 | Heavily apply the rear brake.
On most bikes, squeezing the brake lever by your right hand will apply the rear brake. Do so as you ride downslope to maintain control of the bike. If you do not brake sufficiently, you risk "bombing," or speeding out of control down the rock face. Apply the brakes enough to maintain a speed that enables you to see oncoming obstacles in your path.

5 | Feather the front brake.
Using your left hand (on most bikes), gently apply the front brake as you climb obstacles, and release it to maintain momentum as you overcome them. This gentle apply-and-release action is called "feathering." Avoid applying the front brake suddenly and with full force or the bike will stop short and you will pitch over the handlebars.

6 | Keep the bike in the middle-to-low gear range.
Low gears are easier to pedal; high gears are harder. The gear should be low enough that you can pedal easily over an obstacle, but not so low that you don't have any traction. It should not be so high that surmounting an obstacle becomes difficult or impossible.

7 | Shift your weight.
As you approach large rocks and boulders, shift your body back to take the weight off the front wheel. This shift will allow the front wheel to more easily ride up and over the obstruction.

8 | **Keep your knees and elbows bent.**
Bend your knees and elbows to absorb shocks and to make fast, fluid position changes easier.

9 | **Bail if you lose control.**
If you feel yourself gaining sudden momentum and you begin to lose control, do not attempt to stay with the bike: You do not want to crash while riding at high speed. Let the bike drop out from beneath you, guiding it so it lands on the non-derailleur side to minimize damage that might make the bike unrideable. Tuck your elbows and knees in as you roll to safety.

HOW TO LAND A HANG GLIDER IN A WIND SHEAR

A wind gradient or "shear" is the boundary between two air masses moving at different velocities. The shear will stall the glider or produce extreme turbulence, making it difficult to control. Regain control by increasing speed, which will increase airflow across the sail (the flexible skin of the glider, also called the "wing").

1 Pull in on the control bar so the nose of the glider tilts toward the ground.

2 Shift your weight forward.
This will increase your velocity as you glide toward the ground.

3 Monitor your altitude.
Your variometer (a small computer strapped to the control bar) indicates your altitude in feet. You will probably be at a few thousand feet, descending quickly.

4 Monitor your airspeed.
Check the variometer for your speed. Your "VNE" (velocity never to exceed) on a hang glider is about 50 mph. If you are accelerating rapidly and approaching the glider's limits, pull back on the control bar slightly to bring the nose up and gain a bit more lift.

chapter 6: out and about

5 | Unzip your harness.
As you approach an altitude of 500 feet, unzip your harness so you are no longer in the prone position. Your legs will be hanging down at a slight angle.

6 | Position your hands on the down tubes.
As the glider approaches an altitude of 40 feet, move your hands from the horizontal section of the control bar to the down tubes, which are connected to either side of the bar.

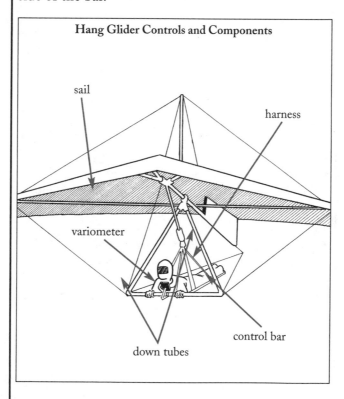

Hang Glider Controls and Components

sail

harness

variometer

control bar

down tubes

7 | Flare the sail.
Push the control bar forward with a smooth, fast motion. The hang glider's nose will pitch up. As the sail angle changes, the air between it and the ground will become compressed and act as an air brake to slow you down.

8 | Land in a standing position.
The glider will have slowed sufficiently to make a stand-up landing possible. As your feet touch the ground, begin a slow run to maintain control and keep the sail from pitching forward suddenly. If the glider frame has wheels, use them to absorb some of the force of the impact.

9 | Come to a stop.
The glider should settle gently to the ground.

Be Aware

- Many hang glider pilots wear a parachute on their chest to use if they are caught in dangerous turbulence or in a severe updraft that sends the glider above 10,000 feet.
- Carry a lightweight package of dental floss for use in an emergency, tree-based landing. When stuck in the tree, hold one end of the floss and toss the dispenser to rescuers. Instruct them to tie their end of the floss to a rope. Use the floss to pull the rope up, tie off, and climb down.

HOW TO LAND
A PLANE

These instructions cover small passenger planes and jets (not commercial airliners).

1 If the plane has only one set of controls, push, pull, carry, or drag the pilot out of the pilot's seat.

2 Take your place at the controls.

3 Put on the radio headset (if there is one).
Use the radio to call for help—there will be a control button on the yoke (the plane's steering wheel) or a CB-like microphone on the instrument panel. Depress the button to talk, release it to listen. Say "Mayday! Mayday!" and give your situation, destination, and plane call numbers, which should be printed on the top of the instrument panel.

4 If you get no response, try again on the emergency channel—tune the radio to 121.5.
All radios are different, but tuning is standard. The person on the other end should be able to talk you through the proper landing procedures. Follow their instructions carefully. If you cannot reach someone to talk you through the landing process, you will have to do it alone.

5 Get your bearings and identify the instruments. Look around you. Is the plane level? Unless you have just taken off or are about to land, it should be flying relatively straight.

YOKE. This is the steering wheel and should be in front of you. It turns the plane and controls its pitch. Pull back on the column to bring the nose up, push forward to point it down. Turn left to turn the plane left, turn right to turn it right. The yoke is very sensitive—move it only an inch or two in either direction to turn the plane in flight. While cruising, the nose of the plane should be about three inches below the horizon.

ALTIMETER. This is the most important instrument, at least initially. It is a red dial in the middle of the instrument panel that indicates altitude: the small hand indicates feet above sea level in thousand-foot increments, the large hand in hundreds.

HEADING. This is a compass and will be the only instrument with a small image of a plane in the center. The nose will point in the direction the plane is headed.

AIRSPEED. This dial is on the top of the instrument panel and will be on the left. It is usually calibrated in knots, though it may also have miles per hour. A small plane travels at about 120 knots while cruising. Anything under 70 knots in the air is dangerously close to stall speed. (A knot is $1^{1/4}$ miles per hour.)

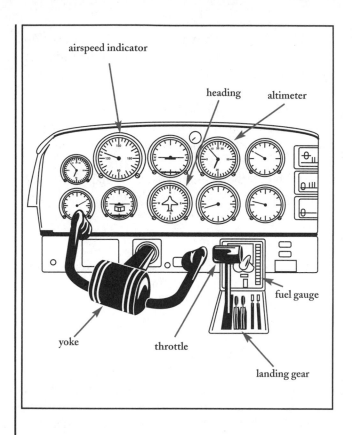

airspeed indicator

heading

altimeter

fuel gauge

yoke

throttle

landing gear

THROTTLE. This controls airspeed (power) and also the nose attitude, or its relation to the horizon. It is a lever between the seats and is always black. Pull it toward you to slow the plane and cause it to descend, push it away to speed up the plane and cause it to ascend. The engine will get more or less quiet depending on the direction the throttle is moved.

Fuel. The fuel gauges will be on the lower portion of the instrument panel. If the pilot has followed FAA regulations, the plane should have enough fuel for the amount of flying time to your intended destination plus at least an additional half hour in reserve. Some planes have a reserve fuel tank in addition to the primary one, but do not worry about changing tanks.

Flaps. Due to their complexity, wing flaps can make the plane harder to control. Use the throttle to control airspeed, not the flaps.

6 | Begin the descent.
Pull back on the throttle to slow down. Reduce power by about one-quarter of cruising speed. As the plane slows, the nose will drop. For descent, the nose should be about four inches below the horizon.

7 | Deploy the landing gear.
Determine if the plane has fixed or retractable landing gear. Fixed landing gear is always down so you need do nothing. If it is retractable, there will be another lever between the seats near the throttle, with a handle that is shaped like a tire. For a water landing, leave the landing gear up (retracted).

8 | Look for a suitable landing site.
If you cannot find an airport, find a flat field on which to land. A mile-long field is ideal, but finding a field of this length will be difficult unless you are in the Midwest. The plane can land on a much shorter

strip of earth, so do not bother to look for the "perfect" landing site—there is no such thing. Bumpy terrain will also do if your options are limited.

9 Line up the landing strip so that when the altimeter reads one thousand feet the field is off the right-wing tip.
In an ideal situation, you should take a single pass over the field to look for obstructions; with plenty of fuel, you may want to do so. Fly over the field, make a big rectangle, and approach a second time.

10 When approaching the landing strip, reduce power by pulling back on the throttle.
Do not let the nose drop more than six inches below the horizon.

11 The plane should be one hundred feet off the ground when you are just above the landing strip, and the rear wheels should touch first.
The plane will stall at fifty-five to sixty-five miles per hour, and you want the plane to be at just about stall speed when the wheels touch the ground.

12 Pull all the way back on the throttle, and make sure the nose of the plane does not dip too steeply.
Gently pull back on the yoke as the plane slowly touches the ground.

13 Using the pedals on the floor, steer and brake the plane as needed.

how to land a plane

The yoke has very little effect on the ground. The upper pedals are the brakes, and the lower pedals control the direction of the nose wheel. Concentrate first on the lower pedals. Press the right pedal to move the plane right, press the left pedal to move it left. Upon landing, be aware of your speed. A modest reduction in speed will increase your chances of survival exponentially. By reducing your groundspeed from 120 to 70 miles per hour, you increase your chance of survival threefold.

Be Aware

- A well-executed emergency landing in bad terrain can be less hazardous than an uncontrolled landing on an established field.
- If the plane is headed toward trees, steer it between them so the wings absorb the impact if you hit.
- When the plane comes to a stop, get out as soon as possible and get away—and take the pilot with you.

HOW TO FIND
WATER ON A
DESERTED ISLAND

1 Collect rainwater in whatever container
is handy.
A bowl, plate, or helmet will work—so will a life raft
and stretched clothing. In very dry environments,
condensation forms on surfaces overnight. Use a tarp
or other fabric—shaped as a bowl—to collect water.

2 Collect dew.
Tie rags or tufts of fine grass to your ankles and walk
in grass or foliage at sunrise. The dew will gather
on the material, which can then be wrung out into a
container.

Tie rags to your ankles to collect dew.

3 | Head for the mountains.
An island that appears barren on the coast may have a green, mountainous interior, which is an indication of freshwater streams and creeks. Find these by following trails of vegetation. Do not waste too much energy hiking or moving long distances unless you are relatively certain you will find water (meaning that the lush greenery is not far away).

4 | Catch fish.
The area around a fish's eyes contains drinkable liquid, as do fish spines (except shark spines). Suck the eyes, and break the vertebra of the spine apart and suck the liquid from them. Fish flesh also contains drinkable water—but fish are high in protein, and protein digestion requires additional water, so you are better off squeezing raw fish in clothing or a tarp to extract water.

5 | Look for bird droppings.
In arid climates, bird droppings around a crack in a rock may indicate a water source. (Birds often congregate around cracks where water collects.) Stuff a cloth into the crack, then wring it out into a container or your mouth.

6 | Locate banana and plantain trees.
Cut down the tree, leaving a stump about one foot high. Scoop out the center of the stump, so the hollow is bowl shaped. The roots will continually refill the stump with water for about four days. The first

three fillings will be bitter, but subsequent fillings will be less so. Cover the stump to keep out insects.

Be Aware

- Seawater is generally not safe to drink; its high salt content can cause kidney failure. Moreover, two quarts of body fluid are required to rid the body of the waste in one quart of seawater. As a last resort, you can drink less than 32 ounces of seawater per day; while not healthful, it may keep you alive.
- Rainwater collected in a container is generally safe to drink, provided the container is clean and the water does not stand; any standing water is capable of breeding bacteria.

How to Open a Coconut on a Desert Island

Drive the end of a stick into the ground and sharpen the top end. Slam the nut down on the point of the stick, using both hands to crack the outer fibrous covering. Smash the inner shell against a rock or tree.

HOW TO MAKE FIRE WITHOUT MATCHES

What You Will Need

- Knife
- Kindling. Several pieces, varying in size from small to large.
- Wood to keep the fire going. Select deadwood from the tree, not off the ground. Good wood should indent with pressure from a fingernail, but not break easily.
- Bow. A curved stick about two feet long.
- String. A shoelace, parachute cord, or leather thong. Primitive cordage can be made from yucca, milkweed, or another tough, stringy plant.
- Socket. A horn, bone, piece of hard wood, rock, or seashell that fits in the palm of the hand and will be placed over a stick.
- Lube. You can use earwax, skin oil, a ball of green grass, lip balm, or anything else oily.
- Spindle. A dry, straight ¾- to 1-inch-diameter stick approximately 12 to 18 inches long. Round one end and carve the other end to a point.
- Fire board. Select and shape a second piece of wood into a board approximately ¾ to 1 inch thick, 2 to 3 inches wide, and 10 to 12 inches long. Carve a shallow dish in the center of the flat side approximately

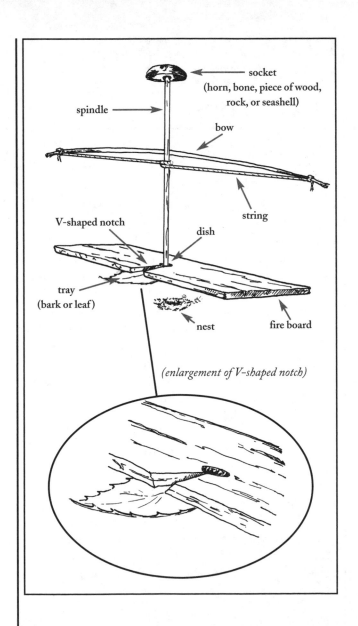

socket
(horn, bone, piece of wood,
rock, or seashell)

spindle

bow

string

V-shaped notch

dish

tray
(bark or leaf)

nest

fire board

(enlargement of V–shaped notch)

$\frac{1}{2}$ inch from the edge. Into the edge of this dish, cut a V-shaped notch.

- Tray. A piece of bark or leaf inserted under the V-shaped notch to catch the ember. The tray should not be made of deadwood.
- Nest. Dry bark, grass, leaves, cattail fuzz, or some other combustible material, formed into a bird nest shape.

How to Start the Fire

1 Tie the string tightly to the bow, one end to each end of the stick.

2 Kneel on your right knee, with the ball of your left foot on the fire board, holding it firmly to the ground.

3 Take the bow in your hands.

4 Loop the string in the center of the bow.

5 Insert the spindle in the loop of the bowstring so that the spindle is on the outside of the bow, pointed-end up.
The bowstring should now be tight—if not, loop the string around the spindle a few more times.

6 Take the hand socket in your left hand, notch side down. Lubricate the notch.

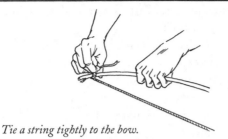

Tie a string tightly to the bow.

Loop the string in the center and insert the spindle.

Press down lightly on the socket. Draw bow back and forth, rotating spindle. Add pressure to the socket and speed your bowing motion until fire ember is produced.

7 Place the rounded end of the spindle into the dish of the fire board and the pointed end of the spindle into the hand socket.

8 Pressing down lightly on the socket, draw the bow back and forth, rotating the spindle slowly.

9 Add pressure to the socket and speed to your bowing until you begin to produce smoke and ash. When there is a lot of smoke, you have created a fire ember.

10 Immediately stop your bowing motion and tap the spindle on the fire board to knock the ember into the tray.

11 Remove the tray and transfer the ember into your "nest."

12 Hold the nest tightly and blow steadily onto the ember. Eventually, the nest will catch fire.

13 Add kindling onto the nest. When the kindling catches, gradually add larger pieces of fuel.

Be Aware

You should not be dependent on any primitive fire method to maintain life in a wilderness survival emergency. Making fire in this manner can be quite difficult under actual harsh conditions (rain, snow, cold).

You should practice this method at home before you attempt it in the wilderness to familiarize yourself with the quirks of the process.

HOW TO SURVIVE WHEN LOST IN THE JUNGLE

How to Find Civilization

1 Find a river.
Generally, animal trails will lead you to water. Water is the key to jungle navigation and usually the quickest way to travel.

2 Fashion a makeshift raft using the method on the facing page.

3 Let the current carry you downstream.

4 Travel on the rivers only during the daylight hours.
Alligators and crocodiles are generally night hunters, so avoid traveling on water at night.

5 Watch closely for signs of villages or settlements.
Many jungle settlements and villages are located along the shores of rivers.

How to Find Food and Water

★ If you do not have the means to purify water, cut sections from large water vines, or cut banana trees (see page 450 for details) and capture the water welling out of the stalks.

To make a raft:

You will need two tarps or ponchos, green brush, two large saplings, and ropes or vines.

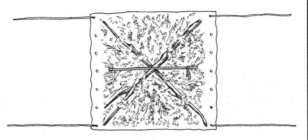

Tie rope to the corners of one tarp. Pile fresh green brush 18 inches high all around. Place two saplings across the brush in an X.

Pile another 18 inches of brush atop the X. Compress the brush. Pull the sides of the tarp tightly around the pile, and tie diagonally.

Place another tarp on the ground. Put the bundle open-side down in the center of the tarp on the ground. Tie tightly as shown. Use the raft rope-side up.

Only drink water from streams and rivers as a last resort, when dehydration and death are a near certainty. Diarrhea will most likely result, so increase your water intake and keep moving.

★ **If you cannot peel it or cook it, do not eat it.**
Avoid brightly colored plants or plants with a milky sap (many of these are poisonous).

Insects, grubs, and raw fish (except those with bristles or spines rather than scales) are safe to eat. Look for grubs and insects beneath rotting logs and vegetation. Pinch the heads off and eat them raw. Peel fruits carefully before eating; the peels may harbor diarrhea-causing bacteria.

How to Travel over Land

- Mark your trail by breaking and turning over fresh vegetation. This will reveal the bright undersides of leaves and will leave a clear trail should you need to backtrack.
- Look for shelter during bad weather. Large hollow tree buttresses can often be used. Line the ground with palm fronds, and stand several more palm fronds over the opening. Note: Do not build this shelter under a tall tree during a thunderstorm because of lightning danger.
- Be prepared for the dangers of the jungle. Most jungle creatures (such as big cats and snakes) want to avoid you as much as you do them. The real danger comes from the smallest creatures: scorpions,

ants, flies, mosquitoes, and the bacteria in water and on fruit. The best defense against bites and stings is to watch where you put your hands and feet. Ants rule the jungle, so do not camp for the night in their line of travel or near nests. Never touch any brightly colored amphibians. Many, like the poison dart frog, have a powerful toxin in their skin, and any contact can make you very ill.

Be Aware

- Before traveling to a remote area, take the time to look at any available maps. Pay attention to topography and any roads or waterways nearby. If you get lost, you will need to know what general direction of travel will intersect a road or waterway and thus, eventually, civilization.
- The jungle canopy can totally occlude the sun, so a compass may be your only means of determining direction. The same heavy canopy will make it impossible for would-be rescuers to find you, or even to locate a downed aircraft. Unlike being lost in a wilderness situation, staying put in the jungle means virtually certain death.
- To make a natural insect repellent, you can use a termite nest. These nests are abundant on the ground and in trees. They resemble irregular-shaped dirt mounds the size of 55-gallon barrels. Break up the mounds (they look like dirt but are actually digested wood) and rub the material on your skin.

How to Drink Water from a Vine

Cut a deep notch in the vine as high up as you can reach. Cut the vine off as low as possible below the initial cut and let water drip into a container or your mouth. When dripping stops, make another cut at the top of the vine and repeat until the vine is drained. This method will work on any vine, though not all vines yield palatable water.

HOW TO LEAVE A TRAIL FOR RESCUERS IF YOU ARE LOST IN THE WILDERNESS

1 Walk through "track traps."
Mud pools, wet sandy areas, snow, and other soft terrain can hold footprints for long periods (days or weeks, between storms). Step in these areas, write "HELP," and draw arrows to signal your direction of travel to potential rescuers. If you reverse course, step in the tracks again on your way out. Your footprints will indicate that the search should not continue past the track trap.

2 Build campfires.
Smoke from campfires can be seen for miles, and fires show up well at night. Warm fire rings also indicate to rescuers that you were recently in a particular area. Do not leave fires burning, but make sure coals or dirt are still warm when you leave. (Warm coals can reignite, so leave warm fire rings only in wet areas or under conditions of low fire danger.)

3 Follow roads and rivers.
Rescuers will use natural boundaries to limit their search area. Do not cross roads or rivers. Rather, follow them to more populated areas. Do not climb steep slopes unless you must: Your searchers will follow, delaying your rescue.

Step in soft terrain to signal rescuers.

Form an arrow to mark your direction.

4 Leave markers.
If you abandon marked trails, signal your direction of travel by turning over fresh vegetation or leaving small piles of rocks.

5 Listen carefully.
In addition to shouting your name, searchers may use a "call word," an unusual word yelled back and forth to distinguish members of the search party from the victim when not in the line of sight. Listen for odd words ("Hoboken," "spaghetti," "Internet") that sound out of place in the wilderness.

6 Yell loudly and make noises in groups of three.
Three calls is the international distress signal. Use a whistle, if available, to signal your position.

7 Sleep lightly.
A rescue party may continue during the night, so use a flashlight or head lamp. Look for flashlights and listen for searchers between naps.

8 Leave personal items behind.
If you are lost in warm weather and have excess clothing or supplies, leave small items along your path as a signal to rescuers. Traveling light will also make hiking easier.

9 Use a mirror to signal to air searchers.
A mirror or other reflective device will help rescuers in planes or helicopters locate your position. Special "survival" mirrors with a hole in the center are especially effective in focusing sunlight.

LAST-DITCH LIQUIDS YOU CAN DRINK

AFTER DISTILLING

- Urine (long-term ingestion can cause problems)
- Blood (human blood may contain hepatitis or HIV, so animal blood is somewhat safer)
- Seawater

AFTER DISINFECTING

- Freshwater creeks/streams
- Toilet tank water (not toilet bowl water), as long as the tank does not have any type of disinfectant, and provided the rubber seal between the tank and bowl is intact and does not leak
- Water from an unknown source

NEVER DRINK

- Ink
- The water in a vinyl water bed
- Swimming pool water (but OK for bathing)
- Water in a hot tub (but OK for bathing)

LAST-DITCH FOODS YOU CAN EAT

cricket

beetle larva

wasp larva

grub

caterpillar

grasshopper

locust

last-ditch foods you can eat

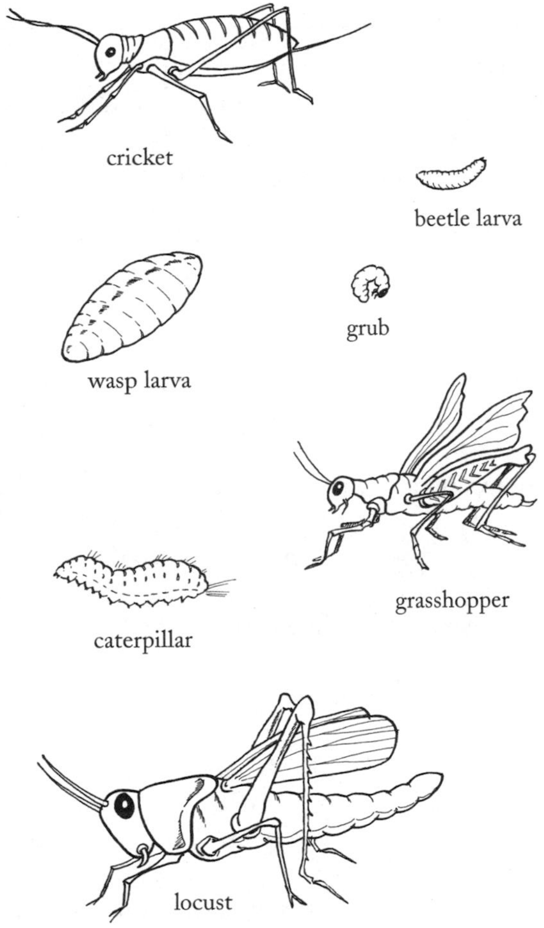

HOW TO SURVIVE IF YOU ARE STRANDED ON AN ICEBERG

1 Construct a shelter.
For protection from the harsh climate, you must build a snow shelter immediately. Your iceberg should have plentiful amounts of snow, so construct either a snow cave (make a huge pile of snow, hollow it out, and crawl inside) or a snow trench (dig a deep channel in the snow, cover the top by stacking snow blocks or improvising a tarp out of materials on hand, and crawl in). A snow trench requires less energy and time to construct, but will limit your range of movement and should be used only if you expect quick rescue.

2 Melt snow and ice to make water.
Place snow in a container and melt over a flame to create drinkable water. If snow is not available, scrape shavings from the topmost layer of ice. Though sea ice contains salt, over time the salt leeches from the ice due to surface melt, and the water from the top ice should be safe for drinking.

3 Cross icebergs to get closer to land.
Wind and ocean currents will keep icebergs in motion, often causing them to crash into one another. Step onto a new iceberg if it will bring you closer to a land mass. Use caution when crossing; the edges may

be very slick, and the ice may be thin and prone to cracking or collapse. Do not jump onto a new iceberg. Test the strength of the ice by pressing lightly with a foot, then adding pressure slowly until you are certain it can support your weight.

4 Catch fish and seabirds.
Fashion a fishing rod with anything available (harpoon, spear, ski pole, or walking stick) and use it for fishing. Seabirds congregate on icebergs, and may be killed with ice balls.

Do not try to reach across icebergs.

5 | Look for seals.
Seals eat fish, and you may be able to scare one away from a fresh catch. As a last resort, if you're not likely to be rescued for a while and can't cross to another iceberg, and only if your life is at risk, consider killing a seal. Seals can serve both as food and as a source of fuel. Unless there is surface melt, without a fuel source you will be unable to melt snow and ice for drinking water and you will quickly die of dehydration. (Avoid sucking on ice: It will lead to hypothermia.) Seals will occasionally jump on drifting icebergs to escape predators and may pop up through breath holes in the ice. While out of the water, seals are generally inactive and docile. Approach adults stealthily from the rear and kill using a club, harpoon, or homemade spear to the skull.

6 | Make fuel from seal blubber.
Cut blubber (fat) from the seal carcass and place in the best bowl you can fashion. Using an implement, pound the blubber until it liquefies. Roll a small piece of material into a wick, place it in the blubber, and light.

7 | Roast or boil seal meat for food.

8 | Burn moist seal skins to create smoky signal fires during the day.
However, your best chance of polar rescue is from land. Just because a ship can see you on an iceberg does not mean it can rescue you.

Be Aware

- Small penguins are also a good food source. Penguins have most of their strength in their flippers, however, so avoid being bashed by a flipper when hunting by approaching from the rear and pinning wings to the sides. Avoid attacking from the front or you risk being badly "beaked."

- In Antarctica, which is a frozen landmass surrounded by ice, icebergs tend to drift in a clockwise pattern around the South Pole, pushed by the circumpolar current. An iceberg may eventually pass a populated weather station or move into a shipping channel. (Weather and research stations may be located hundreds of miles apart in polar regions.) In the Arctic, which is a frozen sea, the currents also move clockwise, east to west, around the polar ice cap. However, the transpolar drift, a current that carries water and ice eastward from Siberia, may bring an iceberg down the east coast of Greenland into more populated areas. The trip from the edge of the Arctic to Greenland may take several months.

how to survive if you are stranded on an iceberg

HOW TO DRIVE IN A BLIZZARD

1 Keep windows clear.
Use the heater, wipers, and defroster to keep windows clear and free of condensation. Do not let the car get too warm, however—the heat may put you to sleep.

2 At night, use low-beam headlights.
High-beams will reflect off the snow, making it more difficult to see.

3 Drive in high gear.
Do not downshift. Use as high a gear as possible for maximum traction and to avoid skids on snowy and icy roads.

4 Drive slowly.
Do not drive at maximum speed. Drive at a slow, constant speed.

5 Avoid sudden movements.
Do not brake, change gears, or accelerate around turns. Slow down and move into a lower gear approaching the turn, then simply steer around the bend.

6 Watch for ice.
Slow down before you reach icy or snowy patches of roadway. Skids are much more likely to occur on ice than on snow.

If You Skid

1 | Undo your last action.
Take your foot off the brake, or ease off the accelerator, depending upon whether you attempted to slow down or to speed up.

2 | Steer into the skid.
To straighten the wheels, turn the steering wheel in the direction the car is moving. Do not jerk the wheel: steer smoothly to avoid further skidding. You may have to turn the wheel in one direction, then the other, to regain control and move straight.

3 | Pump the brake pedal to slow down.
If the brakes are anti-lock, simply depress the brake pedal, and your car will automatically pump the brakes.

4 | Check for traffic.
If you have come to a stop, or if you have spun out of your lane or slowed more than other traffic, you need to be especially careful not to block other vehicles.

If You Get Stuck in the Snow

1 | Turn your wheels from side to side a few times to push snow out of the way.

2 | Place a traction aid under the drive wheels.
Possible objects include a floormat, bag of kitty litter, wood planks, cardboard, a blanket, or clothing.

While driver rocks the car back and forth, time your push to increase forward momentum.

3 **Move passengers above the drive wheels.**
Depending upon whether you have front-wheel or rear-wheel drive, move your passengers and heavy luggage to the front or rear of the passenger compartment. Increased weight over the drive wheels will help to gain traction.

4 **Rock the car back and forth.**
In a low gear, apply light pressure on the gas pedal to move as far forward as you can go without spinning, then release the pedal (or put in the clutch) so you roll back. Gradually, the car will move forward a few more inches with each back-and-forth rock and may gain enough momentum to roll out of its rut and gain traction.

5 | Push the car.
If the car is still stuck, instruct passengers to push the car forward. Try rocking the car back and forth, with a well-timed push at the forward point.

IF YOU BECOME STRANDED

1 | Stay with or in the car.
You can survive for several days in your car, especially if you have food and water and enough fuel to periodically run the engine and heater.

2 | Clear the vents.
The vents for the heater are usually below the windshield wipers on the hood. The exhaust pipe is located under the rear bumper. A clear exhaust pipe allows you to run the engine without danger of carbon monoxide poisoning.

3 | Open a window occasionally.
You will benefit from the fresh air, and will ensure that the windows do not become frozen shut.

4 | If the car becomes completely buried, poke a breathing hole in the snow above the car.
Use an ice scraper or tire iron.

5 | Light a candle inside the car.
If you do not smell any gas fumes, light a candle to provide extra warmth. The candle will also serve as a warning sign of carbon monoxide fumes; if the candle begins to flicker and die, ventilate the car quickly.

6 Put on extra clothing.
To conserve fuel, do not run the engine and heater at full blast. If you do not have enough extra clothing, use newspapers, seat covers, and maps. Huddle with passengers for warmth.

7 Watch for help.
If you have passengers, take turns sleeping so that someone is always alert for possible rescuers. Use a portable radio for news updates; to conserve fuel or your car battery, do not use the car radio.

8 Ration food and drink.
Open and use any useful holiday presents you may be carrying, whether clothing, equipment, food, or beverages. Avoid alcohol, which feels warming but actually lowers your body temperature.

Be Aware
Prepare for a drive in potentially snowy conditions by packing smart. Take extra clothing (including gloves and a water-resistant jacket), blankets and pillows, boots, food and drink, a battery-operated radio and flashlight, matches and candles, a mobile phone, and several wooden planks (or a bag of kitty litter) for traction. Also take a shovel, if possible.

HOW TO SURVIVE WHEN STUCK ON AN OPENING DRAWBRIDGE

1 Draw attention to yourself.
Two-leaf bascule drawbridges—those with two movable sections of roadway that swing from horizontal to vertical—will have a bridge "tender" (operator) in the control house who should be able to stop the opening. Flash your headlights and honk your horn repeatedly to attract his attention so he will lower the drawbridge. If the bridge tender cannot see you (his view may be blocked by one of the open spans) or is not paying attention, you will have to proceed on your own.

2 Back up.
Drawbridges take several minutes to open fully. If the opening span is still relatively horizontal, back up off the bridge (or at least as far back as you can).

3 Get out.
Place your car in gear (or in park if it has an automatic transmission) and apply the emergency brake. Get out of the car and move away: Even with the brake on, the vehicle will begin sliding backward by the time the roadway opens about 30 degrees.

4 | Hold on.
The bridge should have some type of railing and/or a grated road surface that offers hand- and footholds. If a railing is present, grab one of the vertical (fast becoming horizontal) railing supports. Wrap both your arms around the section and grasp your belt, if you're wearing one. If the road surface is grated, face it, place your hands in the grate, and hold on. Drawbridges typically take several minutes to open completely, giving you time to brace yourself.

5 | Wait.
Depending on the height of the vessel moving under the bridge, the span may not move to a completely vertical position. Even in its fully open condition, however, the span will not move beyond 90 degrees, so you will not be hanging upside down. Wait until the ship passes and the bridge span lowers, then walk off the bridge. Your car will have slid down the open span and crashed into the joint where it meets the horizontal section of the roadway.

6 | If you begin to lose your grip or cannot find a hand-hold, jump.
Though any high fall into water should be considered only as a last resort, you stand a better chance of avoiding major injury when landing in water than landing on the road surface. Because the bridge is over a shipping channel, the water below you should be deep enough for you to avoid hitting the bottom. Look down to make sure the ship is not directly below

the bridge, then jump as soon as you can, before the opening span adds elevation to your leap and before the ship is so close that you cannot get out of its way. Keep your legs and feet together, point your toes, and place your arms straight above your head.

7 After breaking the surface, open your arms and legs wide to slow your descent.

8 Head for shore.
Immediately swim up and away from the path of the approaching ship as fast as you can.

Face the grated roadway and hold on.

HOW TO
DELIVER A BABY
IN A TAXICAB

Before you attempt to deliver a baby, use your best efforts to get to a hospital first. There really is no way to know exactly when the baby is ready to emerge, so even if you think you may not have time to get to the hospital, you probably do. Even the "water breaking" is not a sure sign that birth will happen immediately. The water is actually the amniotic fluid and the membrane that the baby floats in; birth can occur many hours after the mother's water breaks. However, if you leave too late or get stuck in crosstown traffic and you must deliver the baby on your own, here are the basic concepts.

1 Time the uterine contractions.
For first-time mothers, when contractions are about three to five minutes apart and last forty to ninety seconds—and increase in strength and frequency—for at least an hour, the labor is most likely real and not false (though it can be). Babies basically deliver themselves, and they will not come out of the womb until they are ready. Have clean, dry towels, a clean shirt, or something similar on hand.

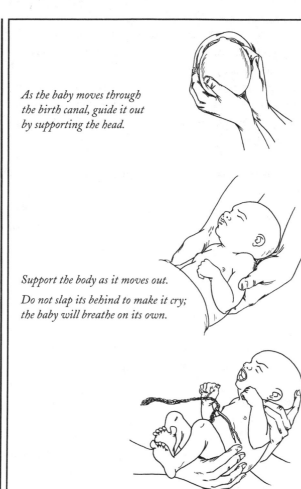

As the baby moves through the birth canal, guide it out by supporting the head.

Support the body as it moves out.

Do not slap its behind to make it cry; the baby will breathe on its own.

After you have dried off the baby, tie the umbilical cord with a shoelace or a piece of string several inches from the body.

Leave the cord alone until the baby gets to the hospital.

2 | As the baby moves out of the womb, its head—
the biggest part of its body—will open the cervix so
the rest of it can pass through.
(If feet are coming out first, see facing page.) As the
baby moves through the birth canal and out of the
mother's body, guide it out by supporting the head
and then the body.

3 | When the baby is out of the mother, dry it off and
keep it warm.
Do not slap its behind to make it cry; the baby will
breathe on its own. If necessary, clear any fluid out of
the baby's mouth with your fingers.

4 | Tie off the umbilical cord.
Take a piece of string—a shoelace works well—and
tie off the cord several inches from the baby.

5 | It is not necessary to cut the umbilical cord, unless
you are hours away from the hospital.
In that event, you can safely cut the cord by tying it
in another place a few inches closer to the mother and
cutting it between the knots. Leave the cord alone
until you get to a hospital. The piece of the cord
attached to the baby will fall off by itself. The pla-
centa will follow the baby in as few as three or as
many as thirty minutes.

If the Feet Come First

The most common complication during pregnancy is a breech baby, or one that is positioned so the feet, and not the head, will come out of the uterus first. Since the head is the largest part of the baby, the danger is that, if the feet come out first, the cervix may not be dilated enough to get the head out afterward. Today, most breech babies are delivered through cesarean sections, a surgical procedure that you will not be able to perform. If you have absolutely no alternatives (no hospital or doctors or midwives are available) when the baby begins to emerge, you can try to deliver the baby feet first. A breech birth does not necessarily mean that the head won't be able to get through the cervix; there is simply a higher possibility that this will occur. Deliver the baby as you would in the manner prescribed above.

HOW TO DEAL WITH A CANCELED FLIGHT

1 Do not stand in line.
When a flight is canceled, for any reason, hundreds of people line up at the ticket counter for rebooking. Ignore them and find a telephone.

Do not stand in line at the ticket counter. Locate a telephone and call the airline to book a new flight.

2 | Call the airline.
Ask the airline (or your travel agent) for a seat on the next flight going to your destination. You will get into the airline's computer system quickly, without having to stand in line. Your airline may be able to transfer your ticket to another flight on that airline, in which case you can proceed directly to the gate.

3 | Book a new flight.
Carry a list of all airlines that fly to your destination. The airline on which you are ticketed may not be able to rebook you on a later flight, or might not be the airline with the next available flight. Call other airlines and book a seat on a convenient flight. Depending on the fare you originally purchased and its restrictions, it might be simpler and faster to purchase a new ticket on a different airline, over the phone, and not use your original ticket. If you purchase a new ticket, proceed directly to the new airline's gate.

4 | Have your ticket endorsed.
If you have made a reservation on a different airline but have not purchased a new ticket, you will need to get your existing ticket endorsed over to the new carrier. You will have to stand in line at the counter of the airline that canceled the flight, but you, unlike others in line, will already have another flight arranged.

5 | Save unused tickets.
Unused tickets, one-way or round-trip, are almost as good as cash: They can be credited toward another flight on the same airline or, in some cases, refunded.

Be Aware

- When flying within the United States, know Rule 240, which covers what an airline will do for you in the event of a flight delay or cancellation. Legally, airlines must compensate only ticketed passengers who arrive on time but are denied a seat. In the event of a lengthy flight delay or cancellation, airlines as a matter of good public relations generally will provide passengers a hotel, meal, free phone call, and other amenities (be sure to ask if they're not offered) or arrange flights on another airline. Check each airline's website for their cancellation/delay policies.

- If you know you will be traveling on a busy holiday weekend to a very busy airport, and especially if there is the possibility of severe weather, book a room in an airport hotel; you will be ready if your flight is canceled. Check the hotel's cancellation policy, so you are not charged for an unused room, and be sure to cancel the room if you don't need it.

- Do not use electronic tickets if there is a chance of bad weather, labor problems, or security delays. The computer systems of different airlines cannot communicate with one another, so e-tickets cannot be endorsed from one airline to another. A paper ticket must first be issued, extending the amount of time you will have to spend at the ticket counter.

- Carry on your bags whenever possible. If your luggage has been checked through to your final destination but you encounter delays, you may not be able to switch your luggage's flights and airlines as easily as your own.

How to Survive a Filthy Hotel Room

Do not come into direct contact with red hazard areas.

HOW TO SURVIVE
A TWO-WAVE
HOLD-DOWN

A two-wave hold-down occurs when a surfer falls off a surfboard while riding a large wave and is held under water for two successive waves.

1 **Bail your board.**
If you are in the impact zone (the area where the lip of the wave meets the trough), dive off your board.

2 **Avoid the "washing machine."**
The washing machine, the white water that occurs as the wave crashes, is turbulent, full of air, and difficult to pierce and swim in. Attempting to surface through it will extend your hold-down.

3 **Do not struggle.**
Fighting a very big (or "rogue") wave will quickly exhaust you and increases your risk of drowning. Remember to "think before you sink."

4 **Dive.**
Swim as deep as you can. Big-wave leashes (the rope that connects you to your floating board) may be 20 feet long, allowing you to go very deep.

5 **Allow the first wave to pass over you.**

leash

Stay down to wait out the wave set.
Follow your leash to the surface.

6 | Locate the board's leash.
If you are disoriented and unable to determine which way is up, grab your ankle and "follow your leash." Since the leash is attached to your floating surfboard, it will lead you to the surface.

7 | Swim toward the surface.
As you approach the surface, place your hands above your head. Your surfboard may be "tombstoning," with its tail submerged and its nose pointing to the sky. Positioning your arms above your head will protect you from hitting your surfboard, a Jet Ski, or another wiped-out surfer as you come up for air.

8 | Wait out the set of waves by diving underneath them.
Waves typically come in sets of three to five, depending on the day and surf conditions. Count the waves as they break so you'll know when the water will calm. Swim as deep as you can and curl your body into a defensive ball as the waves pass overhead. Come up for a quick breath between each wave, if possible, as you wait for the set to subside.

9 | Paddle to calmer water.
When the set has passed, swim to the surface. Climb on your surfboard and paddle as fast as you can farther out to sea, beyond the impact zone, or into the "channel," the blue water that is sometimes to the left or right of the white water.

Be Aware

- Never position your surfboard between your body and a big wave: It will smash into you.
- Never put your back to the waves unless you are paddling to catch a wave and ride it.
- A big wave may hold you down for more than 30 seconds.

How to Survive Sand
in Your Swimsuit

Wade into the ocean. Pull your suit away from your body, jump up and down, and shimmy from side to side to allow trapped sand to be washed away.

HOW TO SURVIVE
A RIPTIDE

Riptides, or rip currents, are long, narrow bands of water that quickly pull any objects in them away from shore and out to sea. They are dangerous but are relatively easy to escape.

1 Do not struggle against the current.
Most riptide deaths are caused by drowning, not the tides themselves. People often exhaust themselves struggling against the current, and cannot make it back to shore.

2 Do not swim in toward shore.
You will be fighting the current, and you will lose.

3 Swim parallel to shore, across the current.
Generally, a riptide is less than 100 feet wide, so swimming beyond it should not be too difficult.

4 If you cannot swim out of the riptide, float on your back and allow the riptide to take you away from shore until you are beyond the pull of the riptide.
Rip currents generally subside 50 to 100 yards from shore.

5 Once the riptide subsides, swim sideways and back to shore.

To escape a rip current, swim parallel to shore until you are beyond the pull of the rip current.

(Direction of rip current)

Be Aware

- Riptides occur more frequently in strong winds.
- Streaks of muddy or sandy water and floating debris moving out to sea through the surf zone are signs that riptides are present, as are areas of reduced wave heights in the surf zone and depressions in the beach running perpendicular to shore.

HOW TO SURVIVE
A TSUNAMI

A tsunami (from the Japanese word meaning "harbor wave") is a series of traveling ocean waves of extremely long length generated by geological disturbances such as earthquakes, underwater volcanic eruptions, and landslides. They can form hundreds or even thousands of miles away. The waves have been known to range from 50 to 100 feet in height. (Tsunamis are often mistakenly referred to as tidal waves, but they are not the same thing. Tsunamis are not related to the gravitational forces which cause tides and, therefore, tidal waves.)

1 **If you are near the ocean, be aware of the warning signs of an approaching tsunami:**
- Rise or fall in sea level
- Shaking ground
- Loud, sustained roar

2 **If you are on a boat in a small harbor and you have sufficient warning of an approaching tsunami, move it quickly.**
Your first choice should be to dock and reach high ground. Your second choice is to take your boat far into open water, away from shore where it might be thrown into the dock or the land. Tsunamis cause damage when they move from deeper to more shallow waters; the waves back up against one another at the shallow shelf. Often tsunamis are not even felt in deep water.

3 If you are on land, seek higher ground immediately. Tsunamis can move faster than a person can run. Get away from the coastline as quickly as possible.

4 If you are in a high-rise hotel or apartment building on the coastline and you do not have enough time to get to higher ground away from the shore, move to a high floor of the building.
The upper floors of a high-rise building can provide safe refuge.

Be Aware
- The first tsunami wave may not be the largest in the series of waves.
- Tsunamis can travel up rivers and streams that lead to the ocean.
- Flooding from a tsunami can extend inland 1,000 feet or more, covering large expanses of land with water and debris.

APPENDIX

THE "IT'S NOT YOU, IT'S ME" LETTER

Dear _____,

    I won't be able to make it this Saturday, or any Saturday, in fact. The truth is, I just can't be in a committed relationship right now. It's not you, it's me. I'm just not able to appreciate all that you have to give.

    I feel like we've been spinning our wheels these last few years / months / weeks / days. I can't believe how wonderful you've been to me and how much you've put up with. You deserve better. I can't put you though this anymore and I can't give you what you need / want / deserve right now. I need more space, and I need time to figure out who the real [*your name here*] is.

    It may take some time, but I hope we can still be friends.

Sincerely,

[*your name here*]

For short-term relationships, this letter may be sent via fax or e-mail.
To download the latest version, visit www.worstcasescenarios.com.

HOW TO TELL YOUR PARENTS YOU'VE BEEN EXPELLED

Mom and Dad—I've got something big I need to tell you. Your baby boy/girl is coming home! And not just for a visit this time—for good.

I've decided that college just isn't working out for me. And believe me, I've discussed this with the dean, my advisors, and several professors, so I'm very sure about it. In a while I'll probably be ready to try school again, at another college, one that is a better fit for my strengths and abilities. This just wasn't the right time and place.

Due to a whole tangle of academic rules and regulations—which were part of the problem, actually—you'll be getting a letter from the dean. Officially, of course, he has to come up with some important-sounding explanations and a lot of exaggerated descriptions of what I've done and not done, and reasons for not refunding the tuition.

But that's not important. What is important is that I miss you guys, and I think that it's best if I leave school now. After all, isn't college really about figuring out who you are and want to be?

I love you both very much. Please send a plane ticket and money to the local youth hostel, where I'm now staying. I look forward to seeing you soon.
Love,
Your son/daughter

HOW TO PAD
A RÉSUMÉ

★ **Be descriptive and creative.**
Employ uncommon action verbs to describe your qualifications and experience. Instead of *worked,* say *coordinated, organized,* or *interfaced.* Consult your thesaurus to avoid repetition.

★ **Exaggerate job experiences.**
Describe your previous jobs in the most sophisticated language you can. No job is unimportant. If you worked the drive-through lane at a fast-food restaurant, state that you "interacted with a diverse client base in a fast-paced environment." See the Job Description Euphemism Chart on the facing page.

★ **Quantify your experience.**
If you were a peer counselor or guided new students through orientation, be specific about how many people you assisted. If you have handled money in a work or extracurricular situation, include a specific monetary amount or number of transactions. List your campus activities, no matter how trivial they may seem. Mention leadership positions within your fraternity, groups you have organized, volunteer work, or participation in protests. The more full the page looks, the better.

Job Description Euphemism Chart

What you did:	What you list:
Worked the deep fryer	Acted as sous-chef in popular lunch venue
Bagged groceries	Coordinated order fulfillment
Answered phones	Interfaced with clients
Mowed lawns	Landscaped for private clients
Made beds	Arranged accommodations for a hotel
Dug ditches	Industrial waste facilitator
Waited tables	Managed client relations
Babysat	Child development consultant
Folded clothes in department store	Sales associate in the garment industry
Gas station/ convenience store clerk	Auto mechanic's assistant
Lifeguard	Health and safety supervisor
Washed dishes	Restaurant critic
Lifted boxes in a warehouse	Inventory manager
Centerfold	Centerfold

⭐ **Keep your résumé to one page.**
A single page looks solid and full and makes you look more focused and experienced. Reduce the type size, change the font, or decrease the margins at the top, bottom, and sides to make it fit.

⭐ **Provide information strategically.**
If your grade point average is below a 3.0, do not include it. If you have a strong GPA in your concentration, list only that. List study groups you have led or special projects in which you have participated. If you include hobbies and interests, be as specific as possible.

⭐ **Work your contacts.**
If you or your parents know someone in the company, or if you were referred to the job by an alumnus or another contact, mention it in the first line of your cover letter.

⭐ **Impress with your presentation.**
Buy heavy cream linen or white laid paper and envelopes to create the impression that you are stylish and sophisticated. If you are including a writing sample, put it in a binder. Type the mailing label or envelope. Make sure the paper stock of your envelope matches that of your résumé. If you are e-mailing a résumé, be specific about the job you are applying for in the subject line. Do something to grab their attention, such as "Marketing Assistant position— YOUR SEARCH IS OVER!" Include the résumé as

an attachment to your e-mail and also cut and paste it into the body of your message to make it as easy as possible for your potential employer to read it.

Be Aware

• Check your spelling. Slowly read your résumé backward to ensure that each word is correct. Pay extra attention to your phone number and contact information.

• Make sure you have a professional-sounding outgoing phone message and that you check your e-mail account regularly. If you live in a group situation, list your cell phone number instead of your home telephone to avoid a roommate answering the phone inappropriately or failing to deliver a message.

JARGON BINGO

Photocopy the Jargon Bingo cards on this spread, cut along the dotted lines, and take the cards with you to your next meeting. Keep one for yourself, and give the others to colleagues. Check off each word or phrase as it is used during the meeting. If you complete a row (across, up and down, or diagonally), you've won! Signal your fellow players by flipping your pen in the air and touching your index finger to your nose.

brand management	optimize	buzz	guerrilla	no-brainer
takeaway	zero-sum	outside the box	slippery slope	team player
killer app	do the heavy lifting	★	ballpark	step up to the plate
up the flagpole	fast track	outsource	tipping point	viral
metrics	big picture	put to bed	downmarket	paradigm shift

blue sky	dog and pony show	game plan	merch	deliverable
upmarket	synergize	quality-driven	check with accounting	empower
facilitate	brainstorm	★	backburner	marketing hook
value-driven	fast track	impulse priced	profit-driven	win-win
user-friendly	proactive	counter-intuitive	revisit	incentivize

re-prioritize	quality-driven	crash	big picture	brainstorm
team player	test case	perceived value	zero-sum	empower
ballpark	facilitate	★	repurpose	brand management
market-driven	backburner	optimize	check with legal	no-brainer
slippery slope	outside the box	fast track	takeaway	upmarket

THE "THERE IS NO SANTA CLAUS" SPEECH

Son/Daughter, please sit down over here by me. There's something I've been meaning to tell you for a long time, and I think you're old enough now.

I know you believe with all your heart that there is a person called Santa Claus who brings you presents every year if you are good. But the truth is that there is no Santa Claus. "Santa Claus" is really all the parents in the world, who love their children very much and buy them presents to show how much they love them.

Your presents are not made by elves in a toy shop at the North Pole. There is no such thing as an elf; and the North Pole is actually one of the loneliest and most desolate places on Earth. The truth is that mom and dad buy all your presents at the mall, and we're the ones who eat Santa's cookies and drink Santa's milk. Reindeer can't fly, either.

But don't cry. This doesn't mean that the spirit of Santa Claus isn't real. "Santa Claus" is inside all of us, whenever we give presents to those that we love or those who are less fortunate. When you grow up, you can be Santa, too. Or the Easter Bunny. Or the Tooth Fairy.

the complete worst-case scenario survival handbook

THE "BIRDS-AND-BEES" SPEECH

Son/Daughter, I think you're old enough now to understand some things about Nature and how we all got here. It's best that you hear about these things from me and not from the kids at school who might not understand everything. I'll explain things to you, and you can talk to me without feeling embarrassed.

You've noticed that there are differences between boys and girls, between moms and dads, and soon you will notice that your body is changing. These changes are normal, and have to do with hormones that your body produces. These hormones and changes are the way your body gets ready to become an adult and to be able to make a baby.

It takes both a man and a woman to make a baby, just the way it takes a male dog and a female dog to make puppies. The female dog has a litter, which means she gives birth to several tiny puppies at the same time. Other animals have babies by laying eggs, but it still takes a male chicken, called a rooster, and a female chicken, called a hen, to produce eggs that have chicks inside. Hens can produce eggs without a rooster, like the eggs we have for breakfast, but those eggs aren't fertilized, which means that they don't have a chick inside and they won't hatch. All birds lay eggs. Female bees and fish also lay eggs, but the way the male fertilizes the eggs is different.

I think that's enough for one day.

Any questions?

ABOUT THE AUTHORS

Joshua Piven is the coauthor, along with David Borgenicht, of all the *Worst-Case Scenario Survival Handbooks*. He lives in Philadelphia with his family.

David Borgenicht is a writer and publisher who lives with his family in Philadelphia. He and Joshua Piven are coauthors of all the books in the *Worst-Case Scenario Survival Handbook* series.

Jim Grace is coauthor of *The Worst-Case Scenario Survival Handbook: Golf.*

Sarah Jordan is coauthor of *The Worst-Case Scenario Survival Handbook: Parenting* and *The Worst-Case Scenario Survival Handbook: Weddings.*

Piers Marchant is coauthor of *The Worst-Case Scenario Survival Handbook: Life* and *The Worst-Case Scenario Almanac: History.*

Jennifer Worick is coauthor of *The Worst-Case Scenario Survival Handbook: College* and *The Worst-Case Scenario Survival Handbook: Dating & Sex.*

Brenda Brown is an illustrator and cartoonist whose work has been published in many books and publications, including *The Worst-Case Scenario* series, *Esquire*, *Reader's Digest*, *USA Weekend*, *21st Century Science & Technology*, the *Saturday Evening Post*, and the *National Enquirer*. Her website is www.webtoon.com.

THE FIRST OF THE WORST

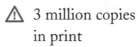 3 million copies in print

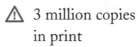 Translated into 27 languages

 International best-seller

"An armchair guide for the anxious."
—*USA Today*

"The book to have when the killer bees arrive."
—*The New Yorker*

"Nearly 180 pages of immediate action drills for when everything goes to hell in a handbasket."
—*Soldier of Fortune*

"This is a really nifty book."
—*Forbes*

A BOOK FOR EVERY DISASTER

⭐ *The Worst-Case Scenario Survival Handbook*

⭐ *The Worst-Case Scenario Survival Handbook:* **Travel**

⭐ *The Worst-Case Scenario Survival Handbook:* **Dating & Sex**

⭐ *The Worst-Case Scenario Survival Handbook:* **Golf**

⭐ *The Worst-Case Scenario Survival Handbook:* **Holidays**

⭐ *The Worst-Case Scenario Survival Handbook:* **Work**

⭐ *The Worst-Case Scenario Survival Handbook:* **College**

⭐ *The Worst-Case Scenario Survival Handbook:* **Weddings**

⭐ *The Worst-Case Scenario Survival Handbook:* **Parenting**

⭐ *The Worst-Case Scenario Book of* **Survival Questions**

⭐ *The Worst-Case Scenario Survival Handbook:* **Extreme Edition**

⭐ *The Worst-Case Scenario Survival Handbook:* **Life**

⭐ *The Worst-Case Scenario Almanac:* **History**

⭐ *The Worst-Case Scenario Almanac:* **Great Outdoors**